# 5 STEPS TO REAL ESTATE SUCCESS

## WHAT EVERY SUCCESSFUL REAL ESTATE AGENT NEEDS TO KNOW TO BEAT THE COMPETITION

LAUREN STARKEY

Library of Congress Cataloging-in-Publication Data
Starkey, Lauren B., 1962–
   5 steps to real estate success : what every successful real estate
agent needs to know to beat the competition / Lauren Starkey.
      p.  cm.
   ISBN 1-57685-480-9
   1. Real estate business. 2. Success in business. I. Title: Five
steps to real estate success. II. Title.
   HD1375.S72 2005
   333.33'023'73—dc22

                                        2004027790


Printed in the United States of America

9 8 7 6 5 4 3 2 1


For information on LearningExpress, other LearningExpress products,
or bulk sales, please write to us at:
   LearningExpress
   55 Broadway
   8th Floor
   New York, NY 10006


Or visit us at:
   www.learnatest.com

# CONTENTS

# ABOUT THE AUTHOR

Lauren Starkey is a writer and editor who specializes in educational and reference works. Her twelve years of experience include eight years on the editorial staff of the Oxford English Dictionary. The author of more than ten volumes, Lauren lives in Essex, Vermont with her husband and three children. She would like to thank the many agents from across the country who shared their insights with me. Their experiences and expertise shaped this book. Every reader of 5 *Steps to Real Estate Sales Success* will benefit from the wisdom of agents from California to Maine, Florida to Michigan, whose combined experience totals more than two centuries.

# INTRODUCTION

This book is intended to help real estate agents in two ways. First, selling real estate can seem like an overwhelming and complicated process. However, by breaking down that process into five distinct steps that directly follow one another, it becomes more manageable. Learning new information piece by piece, in an organized way, makes it easier to understand and master.

Second, while every agent can benefit from being better educated about the selling process, education takes time. And every broker will tell you that, even if you've just gotten your license and aren't sure how to proceed, it's important to simply get out there and start selling. That is why this book is packed with tips from highly successful real estate professionals. These tips can be acted upon immediately, giving the reader dozens of ways to improve his or her business *today*.

*5 Steps to Real Estate Sales Success* will guide you from your first days and weeks on the job to the closing table. Along the way, you will gain the advice of over two centuries of combined sales experience.

In **Step 1**, the different types of real estate offices are compared and contrasted to help you make an informed decision about where to work. In addition, issues such as dealing with personal finances and your support system are examined.

In **Step 2**, you will learn the skills every REALTOR® needs to be successful. Since you have already chosen this exciting field, you probably have many of these skills. But looking closely at how they work to your advantage, and how to improve upon them, helps to take those skills to the next level.

**Step 3** is about what has been called the number one tool for agents, the computer. There is no excuse for being left behind as technology evolves and changes the way real estate business is conducted. More and more buyers look to the Internet to find homes, and the agents who will show them those homes. There is no easier way to keep in touch with your growing client list than by e-mail. By maximizing your knowledge of computers and their application to real estate sales, your marketing of both yourself and your listings will improve, you'll be better organized, and you'll keep up with the latest research and market trends.

**Step 4** examines the issues facing buyers' and sellers' agents. Learn how to deal with first-time buyers, and what a seller wants to hear in a listing presentation. When you understand the needs of buyers and sellers, and how best to meet them, you end up with satisfied customers. Satisfied customers can bring you more business, either through their own next buy or sale or through referrals.

In **Step 5**, the sale moves from contract to closing. Along the way, you will learn how to present offers, get great negotiating tips from the pros, and find out options for dealing with low appraisals. You will also hear about the closing itself, and how to ensure that the transaction goes smoothly.

As one of the most successful agents in New England for over 25 years notes, "You can never have all the answers, so you need to know where to find them." Take Nancy Lang's advice, and turn the page. The keys to your sales success are in this book.

# UNDERSTAND THE BASICS

REAL ESTATE SUCCESS BEGINS WITH FINDING THE
RIGHT PLACE FROM WHICH TO BEGIN YOUR CAREER.
SHOULD YOU WORK FOR AN OFFICE IN YOUR COMMU-
NITY, OR RELOCATE? WHICH TYPE OF REAL ESTATE
OFFICE SHOULD YOU CHOOSE? ONCE YOU BEGIN SELLING,
EXPERIENCED AGENTS AGREE THAT, OTHER THAN HARD
WORK, THE MOST IMPORTANT FACTOR IN YOUR SUCCESS
IS MAINTAINING A REALISTIC VISION OF WHAT YOU CAN
ACCOMPLISH. WHEN YOU KNOW WHAT TO EXPECT,
BOTH OF THE FIELD AND OF YOUR EFFORTS, YOU WON'T
BE DISAPPOINTED. THE REALITIES OF BEGINNING A
CAREER IN REAL ESTATE CAN BE DAUNTING, BUT THEY
CAN BE CHALLENGING AND REWARDING, TOO.

Before you get your first listing, or show your first property, you can make decisions that will set you on the path to success. The first is deciding where to work. Just because there are dozens of real estate offices hiring new agents doesn't mean it will be easy to find a job. That's because you don't just want a job—you want a great job at an office where you fit in and enjoy a good rapport with the other agents. There are many factors to consider before you make a choice.

The second decision is about if and how you will prepare for your new career. Many agents don't bother to think about the financial constraints of beginning work on commission. They don't plan for long, irregular hours, either. A lack of planning can quickly result in those agents resigning before they can even see their first commission check. Start work in real estate sales with your eyes wide open. Know the realities you will face, and plan for them. In doing so, you'll start your career positioned for success.

# YOUR FIRST JOB: CONSIDER THIS

The good news is that it probably won't be difficult to land your first job. Most real estate offices continually recruit new sales agents to join their ranks. It's relatively inexpensive for them to do so, since salespeople are independent contractors (and thus considered self-employed) who usually receive no benefits. Offices get a percentage of all agents' commissions, so the larger their workforce, the greater their profit. In addition, the turnover of sales agents is high in many real estate offices, so desk space becomes available on a regular basis.

But just because it might be easy to find a job, doesn't mean it is the right one for you. There are many employment options to consider. By doing your homework, and exploring each option, you will be more likely to find the situation that is most comfortable for you, and from which you can do your best work.

## LOCATION, LOCATION, LOCATION

Most experts agree that you should capitalize on knowledge of your local area by joining a company close to where you live. If you've lived there for at least a year, you probably know about the neighborhoods, schools, and other selling points, which you can then pass on to prospective buyers. You have also developed a "sphere of influence"—friends, relatives, and acquaintances who make up your initial group of contacts. They are the people who will help you get the word out that you have entered the real estate field. Your sphere will increase as your, and your initial group's, efforts let even more people know about your business.

However, your current location may not provide you with the opportunity for growth and income that you desire. If this is the case, or you are planning to relocate for some other reason, investigate areas that could afford more favorable conditions. For instance, take a look at the areas of the country that are growing fastest. These are the cities and towns experiencing economic booms. New housing is being built and sold, and existing homes are turning over as people move to these areas for employment in large numbers. Below is the U.S. Census Bureau's most recent list of the ten fastest-growing areas with their population percent change from 1990.

| CITY OR TOWN | POPULATION GROWTH RATE |
|---|---|
| Las Vegas, Nevada | 83.3% |
| Naples, Florida | 65.3% |
| Yuma, Arizona | 49.7% |
| McAllen, Edinburg, or Mission, Texas | 48.5% |
| Austin or San Marcos, Texas | 47.7% |
| Fayetteville, Springdale, or Rogers, Arkansas | 47.5% |
| Boise City, Idaho | 46.1% |
| Phoenix or Mesa, Arizona | 45.3% |
| Laredo, Texas | 44.9% |
| Provo, Utah | 39.8% |

If you are considering relocation, you might also want to look at the areas of the United States in which housing prices are highest. Because your commission is a percentage of the sale price, higher sale prices mean more money in your pocket for each transaction. These areas may also be recommended because they are consistently desirable places to live; the housing markets are thriving, and prices are soaring because large numbers of people move there. Below are listed the five cities or towns with the highest median home values, according to the 2000 Census Report. (In comparison, consider that the national average is $119,600.)

| CITY OR TOWN | AVERAGE COST |
|---|---|
| Sunnyvale, California | $495,200 |
| Cambridge, Massachusetts | $398,500 |
| Santa Clara, California | $396,500 |
| San Francisco, California | $396,400 |
| San Jose, California | $394,000 |

## TYPES OF REAL ESTATE OFFICES

Even if you narrow down your list to the real estate offices in your own neighborhood, you will still most likely have several to choose from. What distinguishes them from each other? On the most basic level, there are several types of real estate companies. The most common are national franchises, large independent firms, and small independent firms. Each has potential positive and negative factors to consider.

### National Franchises

You have probably heard and seen a lot of advertising for national real estate franchises. They focus on building brand-name loyalty and national (or even international) recognition among the buying and selling public, and then pass along that name recognition to each independently owned and operated real estate franchise that uses their national name. The franchise company licenses their name to the franchisee in return for a percentage of that firm's profits. Franchises are currently buying up independent firms at a brisk rate all around the country, reducing the total number of real estate offices.

One of the benefits of joining a national franchise real estate company is the training they offer. These companies normally sponsor educational programs to help new sales agents become successful, and to give experienced agents more advanced selling tips and techniques. They also provide state-required continuing education classes free to their agents and brokers, at locations that are convenient to, or even in, their offices. A broker/owner from Fort Wayne, Indiana says he decided to go with a franchise because of the training and national recognition they offer:

> I've been in this business a long time, and I've seen many independent companies giving up their independence to join one of the several successful national franchises. I guess that was always in the back of my mind as I gathered information about my options. I know I made the right

choice because we are doing great financially and my agents are among the most professional in the business. We take full advantage of all the training opportunities, and I do believe that the training has played a major role in helping our new agents to succeed.

---

Advertising is another primary benefit of working for a franchise. The parent company has millions of dollars available to promote its name in many ways. Beyond the typical print, radio, and television ads, advertising may include sponsorship of sporting events, and a large presence on the Internet, both of which can increase name recognition and revenue. Franchise websites allow searches of their nationwide listings. Prospective buyers find properties that interest them on these sites, and then get directed to a local franchise. Some large companies claim to provide hundreds of thousands of leads to their franchisees in this way.

Franchised offices tend to be more structured than independent offices. This means agents may be required to attend regular sales meetings, remain in the office for scheduled "floor time," and be on hand for other organized events. Working with such a schedule may impede the flexibility of your workday, so consider this factor before applying. The benefit to participating in these meetings and other events is that you can gain valuable information and motivational help.

Another benefit to working for a national franchise is that the cost of doing business is decreased. Many of your office supplies will either be supplied free of charge, or at greatly reduced rates. The parent company can buy in bulk, thereby greatly reducing the price on popular items such as business cards, magnets, signs, and real estate giveaways.

However, there is a price for all of the support given by the parent company. Agents typically receive lower commissions than they would at other types of real estate offices, and there are additional franchise/royalty fees and marketing costs that can be passed on to the individual agent as well. Get specific information about commissions and fees when evaluating a job offer in order to make the most informed decision.

## THE BIG FIVE

Below are listed the five largest real estate franchises in the country. Together, they employ over 355,000 sales agents. Three of the five largest companies, Century 21, Coldwell Banker, and ERA, are subsidiaries of the Cendant Corporation.

**Century 21** (www.century21.com) bills itself as the world's largest residential sales organization. It has over 6,600 independently owned and operated broker offices in over 30 countries.

**Coldwell Banker** (www.coldwellbanker.com) has over 3,500 offices in North America, the Caribbean, Singapore, and Central America.

**ERA** (www.era.com) is made up of 2,600 brokerages across the United States and in 31 other countries and territories.

**RE/MAX** (www.remax.com) is the only real estate franchise still owned and operated by its founders. It has 4,700 offices in over 50 countries.

**Prudential Real Estate** (www.prudential.com/realestate) is owned by the insurance company of the same name, and employs over 40,000 sales associates in 1,500 offices across the country and in Canada.

## Large Independent Firms

Independent firms may have many branch offices in one state, region, or city. They are not affiliated with a national franchise, but rather are owned by an independent party. These firms are similar to national franchises in their organized structure and advanced training programs. However, a major difference is that each real estate office that is owned by a large independent firm is most likely headed by an office manager/broker who is not the owner. By comparison, franchised offices are usually managed by the owner/broker of that office. Therefore, with large independent firms, you face a greater likelihood of an office manager relocating to run a different office or to open his or her own office.

That can be an advantage, as working for such a firm offers more management opportunities. The relatively higher turnover in management means more positions become available with some frequency. Therefore, if you think advancement to an office manager position would suit you, large independent firms could be a better fit than national franchises. Another advantage is that you can get many of the same perks of a national franchise, without having to pay the franchise royalty out of your commissions, such as the benefit of a name that has built up a significant amount of local recognition in your community. For independent companies that have several branch offices, the name recognition factor can prove crucial in a local region.

### Small Independent Firms

Small independent firms have one or two branch offices. Most often, they are run by an owner/broker who employs a handful of sales agents. Other independent firms may instead have one large office, where dozens of agents work. Some independent firms specialize in a particular type of real estate, such as waterfront homes, commercial real estate, or upscale condominiums. They may have become experts in their area of specialization and have built up a name for themselves in their community. These can be good firms to work for if you want to learn their area of specialization or if you want to get into their niche market in a local area.

You may have more flexibility in a small independent firm since it probably won't require as many formal sales meetings or other training sessions for its agents. Often, training will be informal and may consist of a conversation with the broker over a cup of coffee instead of a formal classroom atmosphere. This type of office can be a good fit for someone who wants to work part time or who needs extensive flexibility in his hours and in the demands placed on him by the office. Indeed, independent firms are increasingly encouraging part-time sales agents, as the franchise offices are discouraging them or forcing them out. In addition, smaller firms typically attract agents by offering higher commissions than other types of real estate offices, offsetting the lack of support and marketing by maximizing the profit on each transaction.

## How to Evaluate a Real Estate Office

Your future success depends not only on your professional abilities, but also on the company that you work for. In other words, where you work may be almost as important as how you work. Keeping this in mind, there are a number of things to consider as you investigate the real estate companies you regard as possible places of employment.

### Location

Where is the company located? If you aren't willing to add a long commute into your daily schedule, begin by looking at real estate offices located near where you live. Evaluate each office based on the amount of public contact it encourages. Is the location in a busy place? Does it have a large sign that is easily seen by people driving by? Are there other stores and offices nearby that may encourage foot traffic to the office? Does the building look attractive, and is it easily spotted from the street?

### Inside the Office

As you walk up the sidewalk to the door, how does the landscaping look? Is there any? Can you see through the windows? Is there good lighting on the sidewalk and in the parking lot for evening appointments? As you open the door and walk inside the building, try to view the area immediately inside the doorway as a prospective client would see it. Is there a friendly atmosphere? Does the office project a professional image? You want to find an office that appeals to prospective clients and customers as well as to yourself.

Consider desk space, if you will need to use it at the office. How many desks are there, and how are they organized? Will you have any privacy? Are there shared offices or conference rooms that you can use when customers want to speak to you privately? Some people may not feel comfortable discussing their credit histories or income levels with you in the middle of a large room surrounded by hordes of other agents and customers.

## Teamwork

Nancy Lang, one of New England's top-selling agents for over 30 years, stresses the importance of finding an agency that "encourages and rewards teamwork. Interview at a number of different agencies. Speak with the agents who work there and gauge their willingness to be part of the team. Are there a number of primadonnas who've become ostracized from the other realtors? Ask questions and listen carefully to the answers."

Brenda Eager of the Gold Group in Southgate, Michigan, agrees. "You need to get along with the other agents in your office. When you do, you become part of a group that can help you improve the way you do business. You can bounce ideas off each other, and give kudos for new listings and closings. Yes, it is a competitive atmosphere, but competition can be fun."

## What About Advertising?

This could well be the single most important factor in your decision-making. Effective advertising leads to name recognition, making a company's image common to the general population. If you work for a company that has such recognition, your job is made easier because people will associate you with the quality and success of your company before you even say a word. Today, marketing takes many forms beyond the traditional print, radio, and television ads. Companies sponsor sporting events, music concerts, and stadiums, for example. Your examination of a prospective employer's marketing campaign(s) should include all of these.

Compare the printed advertising from several different real estate companies. What is the overall quality of each ad? Note the type of paper, wording, overall appearance, and approach. Look also at other types of advertising, such as billboards, radio and television advertisements, or a telephone hotline. Investigate each of these areas to see how much of a presence each real estate company has. Advertising can directly impact your business if it is done well, by providing you with leads to both buyers and sellers.

Finally, and probably most importantly, evaluate the quality of each company's website. According to the 2003 National Association of REALTOR's Profile of Home Buyers and Sellers, 71% of home buyers reported using the Internet during the first quarter of 2003, compared with

41% in 2002. Therefore, a strong, professional website isn't just good advertising—it is an integral part of success in the business. National franchise sites are a good place to start. They include property listings, mortgage information, neighborhood searches, and even job listings (see the box on page 8 for their addresses). But even small independent firms can and should have similar sites.

To get an idea of the business a great website can generate, consider that Coldwell Banker reports that its site gets over eight million hits and generates over 180,000 leads each year. When a potential client asks for information, he or she is directed to a local office, which can translate into a listing, a sale, or both for that office.

## REALITY CHECK FOR NEW AGENTS

Beginning a career in a commission-based field that involves irregular hours is more complicated than taking a salaried 9-to-5 position. You can't count on a regular paycheck, or on being home for dinner every night. If you enter the field with eyes wide open, knowing what to expect and planning for those realities accordingly, your chances for success will be much greater.

### FINANCES

The agents we surveyed agreed that becoming a REALTOR® is expensive. Before you start your real estate career, you should have enough income saved to cover your basic living expenses for six months. Even if you are able to sell properties right away, it could take a couple of months from the time you put a buyer and seller together to the time you receive your first commission check. In addition to basic living costs, consider these expenses that should be included in your planning:

✓ **New Clothes**—Everyone you meet is a potential new client, so you should think of yourself as "on the job" at all times. That means developing a casual dress look for life. You probably don't need suits or other dressy business attire unless you work in a major metropolitan area, but check to see what other agents are wearing, and follow their lead.

✓ **Errors and Omissions Insurance**—Some agencies cover this expense for their agents, while others do not. If this responsibility is yours, find out the cost and include it in your financial planning.

✓ **Car Expenses**—Your car payment, if you have one, won't change, but your car usage will increase dramatically. Think of your car as an extension of your office. It will be used to transport clients, and can be a base from which you make calls and keep paperwork in order. It must not only be spotless but also be in perfect running order. Expect maintenance costs to rise substantially, and budget for the extra gas you will use each month.

---

### ACT NOW

Consider signing up for roadside service, such as AAA. Many agents consider it a necessity, because any minor breakdown that ties you up for hours could cost you a deal.

---

✓ **Marketing Costs**—You will be printing flyers and other handouts to give people as you seed neighborhoods or use other techniques to build your client base. This will probably cost at least $1,000, and most likely, more. For more information on promotion costs and ideas, see Step 3.

✓ **Fees and Memberships**—Socializing is part of your marketing plan. Many local organizations and clubs charge dues and memberships fees, so do some research and plan accordingly.

✓ **Childcare**—If you have children, you can't take them with you when you show houses, even if you work from home. You need reliable childcare that is available at a moment's notice.

✓ **Tools of the Trade**—Many agencies provide routine office supplies, but you will need to purchase your own personal computer, Palm Pilot or Day Timer®, and a cell phone. If you already have a cell phone, expect the number of calls you make and receive to grow, and plan for the new usage level. See Step 3 for more information on technology and what successful agents agree are necessary tools of the trade.

✓ **Eating Out**—Being on the road means many meals will be purchased. In addition, the closing of a deal is sometimes celebrated by entertaining clients. No matter your financial situation, you want to appear successful, and that means having the ability to cover costs. You never want to be out with a client and have your credit card refused, or be out of cash.

✓ **Things You No Longer Have Time to Do**—More time on the job means less time to accomplish routine tasks. Make a list of the things you do around the house, such as mowing the lawn, cleaning, changing the oil on the car, and doing laundry. What can you reasonably expect to accomplish before or after work? How much would these things cost to have someone else do them?

✓ **Continuing Education**—This won't affect you immediately, but each state has requirements for maintaining your real estate license. Some agencies pay for, and even provide, continuing education opportunities, while others leave it up to you. Find out the cost and location of classes if the financial obligation for continuing education will fall upon you.

---

### NANCY LANG ON WHY AGENTS FAIL

I hired many agents during the 25 years I had my own firm. They all made it through the interview process and initial training, and I always had high expectations for each one. But after a few weeks of work, I could distinguish between the agents who would succeed, and those who would fail. Inevitably, the ones who didn't make it got too caught up in the problems of their clients. They would make great social workers, but not great REALTOR®s. These agents tried to solve buyers' and sellers' personal problems, and didn't help them make decisions. They forgot that the one problem they were trained to solve—finding the right property—was the one they were hired for in the first place. Empathy and good listening skills are critical for good agents, but you can't lose sight of the real service you can provide your clients.

## SUPPORT NETWORK

It's important to have the support of family and friends when you begin selling real estate. These are the people you can turn to when times are tough, and who expect that you will be there for them as well. But real estate sales success requires a big commitment of both time and energy—including some of the time and energy that your family and friends may have been getting. If the people who are important in your life aren't prepared for what the first months of your real estate career will bring, it can lead to problems.

Brenda Eager, a veteran REALTOR® and top seller from Michigan cautions, "Real estate can be hard on new agents. Anyone starting out in this business needs a backup system, especially if they have young children. You don't really make your own hours—your customers do. If a buyer wants to look at houses after work, your hours start at 5:00 P.M. If a seller has three showings on a Saturday, you work weekends. Have a network in place that helps you keep your life in order. Acknowledge the fact that you will, in the beginning, need a lot of support."

Planning ahead can alleviate many of these problems. The following four suggestions will help you to focus on your new career, rather than on crises at home. They will also keep the important people in your life cheering for your success.

1. **Enlist the support of your friends and family in advance.** Let them know what to expect. If there is anything specific you need help with, ask ahead of time. The more your friends and family feel like they're part of a team helping you to succeed, the more they'll be willing to do. People who care about you will be happy to help as long as they don't feel taken advantage of. Without this advance notice, they may feel ignored, or that you no longer care about them.

2. **Provide a timeline.** Family and friends will be willing to make accommodations for you if they know it is not permanent. If it will be difficult for you to attend traditional family events for the next year, be open about it, stressing the fact that it is not a permanent situation, and that it has nothing to do with your feelings for them. When explaining your time constraints, remember that your commitments go beyond the time spent at the office or showing properties. Real estate success also involves reading and researching, traveling around neighborhoods, taking courses, and participating in networking activities.

3. **Keep in touch.** If you can't attend weekly get-togethers with your friends any more, make time to call them and let them know you still care. An unexpected phone call to your spouse in the middle of the day can let him or her know they are in your thoughts. Make the effort to maintain relationships, no matter how busy you are.

4. **Make time for yourself.** The most successful agents don't work around the clock. They know that down time helps them to recharge. Your "indulgences" will pay off at work, too, where you will have a better attitude, renewed energy, and more focus. Vermont agent Lydia Wisloski points out, "real estate can eat up all of your time if you don't manage it well. Take some time for yourself. It's important to have balance in your life." Jill Birdsall, a REALTOR® in Albany County, New York, goes further: "The only way to have some down time is to schedule appointments with yourself just as you would for your clients."

## THE BIG PICTURE

The first few months on the job will be challenging. You may find it difficult to get used to the untraditional work schedule and lack of a steady paycheck. It is critical that you stay focused on why you chose the field of real estate, and remember that the fast-paced, no-two-days-the-same job will eventually result in commission checks. Successful agents agree on this: The more you put into it, the more your job will reward you financially.

But how do you manage expectations and stay positive and upbeat when you put in long hours and get nothing in return? Instead of dismissing negative thoughts, acknowledge them, and then rethink them. For example:

| | |
|---|---|
| *Negative Thought:* | I'm spending more time at work than with family and friends. |
| *Rethink As:* | My real estate career will bring me into contact with thousands of new people, some of whom may become friends. |

| | |
|---|---|
| *Negative Thought:* | I'm working so hard, and haven't gotten one listing or sale yet. |
| *Rethink as:* | I know that making good money in the first months as an agent is rare. But I have the motivation and drive that will eventually lead to commissions. |

Another technique for dealing with negative thoughts and unrealistic expectations is to focus on the big picture. Why did you decide to enter the field of real estate? Probably because of many or all of the following reasons:

✓ **Excitement**—When you are stressed by long hours that don't seem to be paying off, remember that tomorrow will be another experience. The job changes from day-to-day and moment-to-moment. Real estate is challenging and fast-paced. Not only will your tasks vary, but that way you approach them can, too.

✓ **People**—Real estate will bring you into contact with many different kinds of people, and you'll be meeting new faces constantly. If you like to interact with people, real estate is a terrific field.

✓ **Satisfaction**—Unlike most sales jobs, you're helping people do something they want to do and, in many cases, helping people to dramatically improve their lives. Enjoy the satisfaction that comes from helping buyers to find and purchase their dream house, or helping sellers to financially better themselves.

✓ **Money**—Once you're established, real estate can be a lucrative field. Even a hardworking newcomer can make reasonably good money. According to a recent survey by REALTOR® Magazine, agents with five or fewer years' experience made an average of $27,214. With six to ten years, income jumped to an average of $69,899. The median salary for those with more than 25 years of experience was $82,501. However, regardless of time spent in the field, those with at least one personal assistant earned an average of $123,006. REALTOR®s reported that their personal assistants, whether full- or part-time, earned an average of $23,565 a year.

## To Review

✓ Decide where to sell from. Your town or area of residence makes sense because of the knowledge you already have but, for some people, relocation is a good idea. Make an informed choice about the location of your business.

✓ Working for a large national franchise has many advantages, including training, marketing, and support. Downsides include lower commissions and a more structured work environment.

✓ Large independent agencies offer greater chances for upward mobility. If you think you would eventually like to move into real estate management, while enjoying the marketing and name recognition of a larger firm, this could be a good fit.

✓ Small independent firms offer the greatest flexibility, including part-time work. They also typically pay higher commissions to their agents. However, the costs of doing business, including marketing, supplies, and office spaces, may fall upon you.

✓ You will probably have a choice of firms to decide among. Evaluate them carefully before making a decision, by comparing location, aesthetics and workability of office space, and advertising.

✓ Maximize your chances for success by retaining a realistic picture of beginning real estate sales.

✓ Prepare for the financial realities of the first months on the job, and plan accordingly. You won't see a regular paycheck, and might not receive a commission for many months. You must know the expenses you'll need to cover, and how you'll cover them.

✓ Keep your support network of family and friends vested in your success. As your work keeps you away from home and preoccupied, make an extra effort to maintain meaningful contact with the people who mean the most to you. You will need their support, and they will need you, too.

✓ When the long hours and possible lack of financial compensation get you down, keep your eye on the big picture. Most agents don't make much money during their first few months in sales. Remember why you chose the field, and what your future success will look like.

# DEVELOP SKILLS FOR SUCCESS

While the training you received before licensing is vitally important to your career, it probably didn't teach you about some of the most important elements of real estate sales success. Training concerns itself primarily with the legal and ethical aspects of your chosen field, rather than the skills you will need on your first day, and every day, to succeed as a real estate agent. Dozens of top-selling agents from around the country have been surveyed about those skills that are most important in determining real estate success. While approaches may vary, they all agree that their careers are built on the five skills detailed in this Step.

The easiest way to develop success skills is by first learning what they are, and then breaking them down into manageable parts. When you increase your awareness of what is needed from you, you can work on weak areas, and play up strengths. If shyness is keeping you from cold calling, you could benefit from a class in public speaking, and perhaps also from a new focus on other marketing strategies. If you've always thought of networking as insincere small talk and handshaking, you will benefit from a better understanding of this vital tool for building a client base and developing a professional reputation that will bring you business.

# PERSONAL SKILLS

All REALTOR®s can get a good educational foundation, and thoroughly understand the fundamentals of real estate. But those basics can take you only so far on the road to success. What separates top-selling realtors from those who work hard without seeing much of a financial return? There are six qualities that count the most, according to the experts.

## HONESTY

Being honest in your dealings with other salespeople, your office manager, your clients, and your customers is of the utmost importance. If you aren't, not only will your professional reputation suffer, but there could be legal consequences that could potentially end with your license being revoked. As Don Marcy, a REALTOR® for over twenty years, notes,

---

There is a lingering perception among homebuyers that ours is a cutthroat field where you have to be a real shark to survive. Maybe this was true a long time ago, but today the image of the hot-shot salesman who will say anything and do anything to get the sale is as outmoded as the buggy-whip.

---

## FLEXIBILITY

Remain adaptable in both the scheduling of your time, and in your career plans and goals. What if you are determined to sell only houses and condos, but find the market is weak? Should you give up, or learn all you can about selling land and investment properties? Listings and sales don't come at predetermined times. You might have a month in which almost nothing happens, and then one in which you are inundated with business. Use slower times to review your marketing plan, perform market research, and keep up with local and national trends. If you expect twists and turns, you will be able to flex with them, rather than let them break you.

## SELF-MOTIVATION

Since your success depends on your own efforts, you need to be highly motivated. Your motivation to succeed will give you the energy you need to place cold calls and drum up new business when things are slow. Some agents use motivational tools such as books, tapes, and workshops to keep them energized, while others find interaction with peers, such as through real estate organizations, keeps them on top of their game. Find what works for you, and recognize those times when you need a boost in motivation.

## LISTENING SKILLS

Real estate agents need to listen carefully to the needs and desires of their customers, so they can serve those needs and close the sale. Sometimes your clients may not be able to tell you exactly what they are looking for, so you'll need to ask the right kinds of questions to determine their wants and needs.

Nancy Lang, the first REALTOR® in New England to sell over $1,000,000 in properties explains, "come up with open-ended questions. Don't ask a string of questions that require a `yes' or `no' answer." For instance, instead of asking if they require a master bath, ask about how they see themselves using it. Do they want a relaxing spa area, or are they people who take quick showers and get on with it? If your listening skills are good, you will come up with more questions and answers. Eventually, you will have a much more detailed vision of what your buyer is looking for. They in turn will be pleased that you took the time to listen and understand them. Nancy sums it up, "I became successful when I learned how to listen."

---

YOU KNOW YOU'RE NOT
A GOOD LISTENER WHEN . . .

. . . your listing presentations take more than a half hour.

. . . you start showing properties with just a price; location; and bed and bath count.

. . . you can't get through your prospecting script in less than three minutes.

. . . you spend more time talking about you than you do finding out about your buyer or seller.

. . . you've offended someone at a closing through an offhand remark.

---

## ABILITY TO LEARN FROM MISTAKES

Face up to your mistakes and use them to learn how better to deal with similar future situations. For example, after a meeting with a seller that didn't result in a listing, make note of what went wrong and why to help you overcome that obstacle in your next listing meeting. If your seller finds a mistake in their listing, apologize and fix the error quickly. Then, take a moment to think about how the error occurred. Did you rush to get the listing onto the Multiple Listing Service (MLS)? Were the notes you made while measuring and examining the property too sloppy to read? If you learn from your mistakes, you will perform better in the future.

## TOLERANCE

You never know who your next client might be. A genuine respect for people of all ethnic backgrounds, races, religions, and lifestyles is needed to be able to build rapport with anyone and everyone seeking your services.

# PUBLIC INTERACTION SKILLS

An agent's work revolves around people—sellers, buyers, tenants, mortgage bankers, lawyers, and brokers. In order to get the job done, and gain the trust and respect of those you work with, you need to behave in a way that others will respond positively to. That means being friendly, open, and kind. Keep that mind while interacting with everyone in your professional life.

## LIKEABILITY

Buying a home is not only an enormous financial transaction, but it is a highly personal decision. Buyers and sellers won't want to do business with you if, first and foremost, they don't like you.

---

### THE NUMBER ONE RULE OF BUSINESS

People do business with people they like.

---

Not only will they do business with you, but they may do repeat business with you, or refer other business to you! When clients like you and your services, there is no end in sight to the income they can bring you.

That doesn't mean you won't run into some seriously unpleasant people along the way. Every REALTOR® has a story or two about an impossible client. But what counts in the long run is that you treat even the most difficult people with respect. Try not to second guess someone's motivations, especially when they create negative consequences for you; most of the time, their rudeness or change of heart has nothing to do with you.

## CONFIDENCE

A strong sense of self inspires others to perceive you positively. Confidence adds to your likeability, and it also helps you to stay motivated when you face the inevitable rejections that come with your job. Perhaps you've spent hours with a client, showing her every property in the county that meets her criteria. A week later, you discover that she signed a contract with someone else. Confidence will help you get back in the car and do it all over again with another client.

---

### ACT NOW

Need a confidence boost? Schedule at least five property previews for the next few days, and five more for next week. Then, make it a habit to regularly preview as many homes as possible. Previewing gives you first-hand knowledge of your inventory, and when you're knowledgeable, you gain confidence!

---

## PEER RELATIONSHIPS

Because of the number of other agents working in your area, chances are that your listing will be sold by someone else. Therefore, the number of agents in your area who know and respect you, and the way in which you market your properties to them, can make a big difference in how successful you become. One of the best ways to develop positive peer relationships is to attend every meeting you can. Office, board, and MLS meetings can be time consuming, but you will get a chance to meet many other agents, and get a great understanding of local real estate issues.

On the other hand, these agents are also your competition. They want the same clients, listings, and sales you do. How do you balance the need to be likeable with the need to win?

Lisa Marie Brown, a top-selling agent in Maine, has this advice:

---

It can be very difficult to work with other agents. Some of us are professionals, and some of us aren't. It's important to be very professional, ethical, and courteous at all times. But, it's also important to keep an eye on every part of the transaction. Remember that your license is on the line not only for what you do, but for the actions of other agents you're working a sale with.

---

## TIME MANAGEMENT SKILLS

As an independent contractor with little supervision from superiors, you will need discipline to work on a regular schedule. Just because you can come in late and leave early doesn't mean you should. No one will check to see if you prepared the market analysis you promised for tomorrow, but that doesn't mean your client won't notice.

Planning is the best way to assure that you will use your time wisely, and get everything on your to-do list taken care of. Decide which tasks need to be accomplished every month, and approximately how long it will take to complete each one (if they are ongoing, estimate how many times a month they should be attended to, and for what period of time). Many agents find it useful to schedule time for paperwork and marketing tasks as though they were important meetings. You might put on your calendar a meeting with yourself every Tuesday from 10 A.M. to 11 A.M., when you sit at your desk and work on copy for your next newsletter. Or, on Friday afternoons you regularly contact any new additions to the list of owners who are trying to sell their own properties.

In order to stick to your plan, remember two important points. One, you should first leave plenty of room on your schedule for time with clients. If you're overbooked with yourself, you will find that the plan gets tossed aside too frequently. And two, be able to distinguish between what is urgent and what can wait. While your availability to clients is critical, it doesn't mean you need to drop everything every time someone needs something. Get in the habit of returning phone calls and e-mails within 24 hours. There are a few legitimate emergencies you will encounter, but many clients behave as if their every need is an emergency. By prioritizing, you will make enough time to get everything done when it really needs to get done.

Good time management skills also means spending most of your working hours on those activities that earn you money. Successful agents recommend that about 30% of your time should be spent on marketing both you and your listings. If you find you are spending most of your time showing buyers current listings, you aren't doing enough to generate a steady stream of future business.

Because you have so many different tasks to complete (showing properties, preparing comparative market analyses, attending closings, negotiating, preparing listings, marketing, presenting listings and offers, etc), you can't afford to waste time. That means if you find yourself chatting too much in the office instead of uploading your listings onto your website, you might think about using your home computer instead. One of the biggest time wasters in real estate sales is working with clients who aren't sure they're buying, or who can't afford the homes they want to see. Weeding out the browsers from the buyers, therefore, is an essential skill.

## ACT NOW

Don't waste another minute with browsers posing as buyers. The next time you are on the phone with a prospective buyer, use this script from Lisa Marie Brown, a top-selling agent from Maine:

Lisa Marie (LM): Have you been to the bank yet?

Prospective Buyer (PB): No.

LM: The most important step in buying a home is getting a pre-qualifying letter from your lender. Sellers won't even look at an offer if you're not pre-qualified. I can give you the names of three wonderful loan originators who can help you with this right over the phone. Then you can decide which one, if any, you want to use.

*[insider tip: if it's not in person, and easy to do, they'll do it]*
*[insider tip: make it their decision; you don't want to lead them to one or another]*

PB: When can we start looking at houses? I drove by one today that I really want to see.

LM: As soon as we find out what you are qualified for, we'll start searching for your new home. Some of our sellers don't even want showings to take place if the buyer isn't pre-qualified. So that's our first step. Give me a call back as soon as you have your letter. I know we can find your new home together!

*[insider tip: use the word "we" often, to convey your willingness to be part of their team]*

# MARKETING SKILLS

Marketing, or reaching your target audience of potential buyers and sellers, is a science (in addition to being expensive and time-consuming). If you don't understand how it works, you probably won't succeed. Before you spend any time or money, read this segment carefully. Marketing success comes from planning and then following through with incremental steps, not by jumping in with haphazard mailings and advertisements.

---

### THE FOUR MOST COMMON MARKETING MISTAKES

1. **Seeing yourself as a real estate entrepreneur first, and a marketer second (or third, or fourth).** You will not make money in real estate sales if you don't market yourself. The only way to earn a living is to create (not hope for) a steady stream of motivated buyers and sellers. By seeing yourself as a marketer first, you will prioritize your time accordingly, spending the hours needed to implement a well-thought-out marketing plan.

2. **Jumping in without a plan.** Don't waste hundreds or thousands of dollars during your first months on the job trying various marketing gimmicks. Just because your broker recommends two hours of cold calling a day doesn't mean it is the right marketing tool for you. Develop a plan before spending any time or money on marketing.

3. **Focusing on one-shot deals rather than a process.** Successful marketing is a plan with many steps, which is executed continuously. You're never done with marketing. So spending time on an elaborate give-away or limited-time offer, unless it's part of an overall plan, is a waste of time. You don't build a loyal client base by giving away televisions.

4. **Not giving your marketing a chance to work.** Few
   people respond to an ad the first time they see it. In fact,
   it usually takes more than five times before there is a
   positive response. If your marketing plan is sound, stick
   with it. It's not realistic to expect incredible results in a
   short period of time, because marketing is a process. You
   need to reach your potential client base many times,
   convincing them consistently over time that you deserve
   their business.

## STEP ONE: DEVELOP A UNIQUE MARKETING IDENTITY

You know how much competition you face—not only are there many other
agents in your area, but most of them have plenty of experience, too. Your
primary goal in marketing is to stand out from the competition. But how can
you do that when your experience doesn't come close to theirs?

Instead of focusing on what you can't offer, turn your attention to what you
can. Lead people to perceive you as someone with whom they will want to work
by giving them a positive impression. Present them with an identity that they will
remember and turn to. This identity incorporates both who you are and what
you do (what types of services you provide). Once you've developed it, you will
use it consistently, no matter what type of marketing strategy you choose. Your
identity should be unique, clearly describing how you differ from, and are better than, your competition. Take time to think it through. What personal qualities are your best and strongest? Do you always follow through on every detail?
Are you punctual? Are you trustworthy? Ask friends and family for ideas, and
then chose the quality that works best with your position in sales.

Next, focus on what services you can offer that are both different from and
superior to the competition. Don't choose specifics such as how much you'll
spend on marketing, or how quickly you will sell a house. Your marketing
identity is about eliciting a feeling from your targeted audience. In other
words, instead of telling them about how many houses you can show them in
a weekend, tell them how you will find them a home in which they can
create the family of their dreams, or showcase their wonderful taste, or feel safe

and secure at night. Note that you are describing how your services will benefit them, rather than on detailing the specifics of your services.

---

TOP-SELLING REALTOR® BRENDA EAGER
SHARES HER ADVICE

"If you don't already have a name tag, get one made. It should be good-looking, and preferably magnetic, since it is easier to move from outfit to outfit, and doesn't make holes. It is essential that you wear the nametag unless you are at home, or out with family or friends. Nametags are an icebreaker, and an important part of marketing yourself."

---

Your identity might be a particularly good fit with a specific group. For instance, perhaps you once worked at a local college. You decide your marketing identity is that connection—you have a unique ability to understand the needs of other college employees looking for housing. In an area with many colleges and universities, you will have a huge potential client base to target.

Or, your identity might be cost effectiveness. You might offer a lower commission, or explain all of the additional services you provide for the same fee as others. In all of your marketing efforts, you stress the value of your services. Another approach to creating an identity is to focus on your unique approach to real estate sales. If you've bought and renovated four homes, focus on your ability to see the potential that lies behind neglect or bad taste. Your client base could be young families who want a home, but don't have a lot of money to spend. What they have plenty of, though, is energy to paint, scrape, and landscape.

## STEP TWO: GET YOUR IDENTITY OUT THERE

Once you've established your marketing identity, you need to share it with your market regularly. That doesn't mean putting all of your energy into one newspaper ad. You want your identity in front of your prospects as often as possible. Consider periodically sending out letters or postcards, either through the postal service or via e-mail (see Step 3, page 43, for more information about using electronic newsletters). Be consistent in whichever medium you chose, whether print advertisement, brochure, or letter. Your identity should be recognizable as uniquely yours after a few rounds of marketing.

---

### ACT NOW

Is that stack of expensive brochures still sitting in your office? Call local and regional papers to find out how much it would cost to insert one in the real estate section next Sunday. Some larger newspapers even pinpoint certain neighborhoods for their advertisers. For a reasonable cost, you can get your name, and your marketing identity, in front of thousands of prospective clients this week!

---

Stick with your approach no matter how little response it seems to elicit. General rules of marketing indicate that a prospect needs to see your identity at least six times before it will resonate with him or her. By marketing yourself consistently, you should begin to make an impact in about six months.

In addition to using print materials, these six marketing methods have been used with success by many realtors. As you consider them, think about ways in which your unique marketing identity would fit each one.

1. **Cold calling**—make random phone calls to try to find those who are about to buy or sell a home.

2. **Farming a neighborhood**—blanket an area with information about yourself so that people interested in selling houses remember your name and have a positive image of you.

3. **Open houses**—offer to run an open house for a more experienced, busy REALTOR®. Many people who attend them are about to put their house on the market, and are interested in the competition.

4.   **Organizations**—get involved in activities and community organizations that bring you into contact with many people who share your interests; some of them will be selling houses or will know people who are.

5.   **Expired listings**—approach the owner of a property that another agent failed to sell.

6.   **Referrals**—find sellers among the people you know, and/or the people they know.

---

### IN THE NEWS: A NOTE ON COLD-CALLING

Long considered a staple of real estate marketing techniques, cold calling may become a thing of the past as agents are required to comply with the provisions of the National Do-Not-Call Registry. While legal challenges continue to be brought forth, and fine-tuning of the law occurs, there are federal rules in place that not only supercede the less restrictive state Do-Not-Call rules, but demand a penalty of $11,000 per illegal call. Don't pick up the phone to make a cold call until you understand current laws on the topic.

---

## SECRETS OF MARKETING A PROPERTY

While it's true that your primary goal in marketing is to sell yourself, you will also need to market the properties you list. You know about how to place a newspaper ad, list the property with the MLS, run open houses for agents and buyers—these are the marketing tools every REALTOR® uses. The key to standing out from the crowd is in how you perform those basic marketing functions. Each has particular pitfalls to avoid, and ways in which to use them to full advantage. Understand each one, and fine tune your property marketing efforts to sell more, faster.

✓ **Write a great listing.** This seems straightforward—you simply measure the house and all of its rooms, take note of special features, and plug the information into the computer. You might be surprised to learn how many listings are either incomplete or incorrect. "Take your time," says agent Joyce Kirchner of Florida. "Use a simple form to be certain you don't leave anything out. Fill it out with the help of the homeowner, and ask him or her questions about their property. What is the best feature? Worst? The more information you have, the more accurate and complete a listing you can write."

✓ **Take a great picture.** Prospective buyers' first impression of the property will most likely be a picture. Some agents will even let the buyer scratch a home off their list if they don't like the picture. Know how to use your camera. If possible, take the picture when sunlight shows off the property to full advantage, and be certain it shows the house from the best angle. If you're not sure how to do this, gather listings from some of the top selling agents in your area. Drive by each property, checking the house against its photograph. What works? What doesn't? It is always helpful to take many pictures from different angles. When you get back to your office, you'll have a choice.

✓ **Invest in good signs if your company doesn't provide them.** It is a great way to get your marketing identity out to the public, so you want to be consistent. Joyce Kirchner says, "yard signs lure buyers. But the signs of most independent agents are too small, and they often look cheap. It would behoove a new independent, therefore, to invest in really good design to get a sign with clout. You'll have to pay more for a great sign, but it's worth the expense."

✓ **Target the top-selling agents in your area.** They're the ones selling most of the properties. Make sure they know about your listing directly from you. Put together a flyer, or send an e-mail with pictures.

✓ **Run a well-attended open house.** Open houses for other agents are often scheduled during weekday mornings. Are top-selling agents offering breakfast at their open houses? This is a trend in some areas of the country. Some agents report that open houses with food from certain caterers are better attended than others. Do what works to get the most traffic through the house. Open houses for buyers require a high level of visibility. Don't assume an address is enough to get them to your listing. Use at least three road signs with arrows pointing the way from a major intersection. Balloons are also helpful, as is a large sign on the lawn. The more buyers and agents who see your property when it is listed, the better your chances of selling quickly. For more information on open houses, check out Step 4, page 67.

# NETWORKING SKILLS

Networking has a bad reputation. Many people think of it as the height of insincerity: shaking hands and making small talk with people you don't care about in the hopes that they will help you. If you believe that reputation, you will miss out on one of the best ways to meet, and even exceed, your sales goals.

In order to be a success in real estate, you need buyers and sellers. How do you find them, and get yourself out where they can find you? By networking. But the value of this tool doesn't stop there. Networking is also a great way to keep up with local, regional, and national real estate trends. It helps develop peer relationships. And it helps establish your reputation as a professional in the field.

The previous section on marketing mentioned referrals as a marketing tool. Think of networking as the active way get them. By networking, you don't simply hope that a family member or satisfied client will tell someone about you. You work with that family member or client to help them send business your way.

## ASK FOR WHAT YOU WANT

Use a direct approach. Have you talked to your family about what you are doing? Do *all* your family members know that you are a real estate sales agent looking for clients? Have you asked family members if they know anyone looking to buy or sell a house in your area? Do their friends? Expand your sphere of influence by requesting that family members ask *their* friends.

Do your friends know that you can help them buy or sell a home? Ask them to expand your client base by keeping an eye out for potential clients and actively referring them to you. If your friends ask *their* friends and family if they know of anyone planning on buying or selling a house in your area, you will have created a circle of hundreds of people who know you and are looking for clients for you.

In addition to family and friends, consider the following people as lead generators:

- ✓ former teachers
- ✓ current or past coworkers or fellow students
- ✓ former employers
- ✓ car repair people
- ✓ your children's friends' parents
- ✓ lawn mowers/landscapers
- ✓ mail and newspaper carriers

The idea is to get the word out to as many people as possible that you are a real estate agent. Think of everyone as not only a potential client, but a potential source of clients, as well.

If you are using networking to get information from other agents, it is also best to be direct. Perhaps your current marketing strategy is slumping. You want to find out where successful agents are advertising their homes. You could check all of the local and regional papers, or you could ask. By approaching them first with an acknowledgment of their expertise, you will probably get a straightforward answer.

## Join Local Clubs and Organizations

Participation in local groups, such as the Chamber of Commerce, Junior League, or Lion's Club, is a great way to network. Meetings and other activities will bring you into direct contact with the business people in your town or city. Joining a golf or tennis club, garden club, the local school board, or any other group that interests you, will also widen your circle and help you get the word out about your career.

## Join Online Discussion Groups

If you need help from other agents, but aren't comfortable asking for it in person, there are a number of online communities that can help. For instance, www.groups.msn.com has a "Real Estate Networking Group" and www.yahoo.com has over 1,000 different groups for real estate professionals. www.agentsonline.net has a dozen different discussion forums. These groups offer a level of anonymity, and the chance to get advice or information from hundreds of other agents.

## Professional Organizations: The National Association of REALTOR®s

Another way to network is to join a group of real estate professionals. Not only can you get information to help you with the first months in your new job, but your affiliation with such a group can also help you throughout your career in a number of ways. The National Association of REALTOR®s (NAR) is the nation's largest organization of real estate professionals (as well as the largest trade and professional association of any kind). It was founded in 1908, and currently has over one million members. Members are known as REALTOR®s, and include brokers, salespeople, property managers, appraisers, counselors, and others involved in the real estate industry. They first join one of 1,700 local associations/boards, and membership is then extended to the state and national associations. Members are pledged to a strict Code of Ethics and Standards of Practice (to read it log onto www.realtor.com).

The NAR is active politically, both by financing lobbyists who work to protect its members' interests, and by encouraging the involvement of its members in the campaigns of candidates backed by the NAR. Members have access to industry information and each other through a website (www.one realtorplace.com), a magazine, meetings, and conventions. They can network, find news about changing legislation that may affect their business, and do research at an online real estate library. Roberta Dinerstein, an agent in Boca Raton, Florida, notes that

> The NAR does good work for REALTOR®s, especially by lobbying for our causes nationwide. This does seep down to the state and local levels. For so many years, REALTOR®s had a public relations problem, and I believe that has really improved, in large part due to efforts of the NAR and its individual members.

Membership in the National Association of REALTOR®s has other networking benefits that can add to your sales success. The NAR maintains www.realtor.com, the largest online source of real estate listings. As a member, you will be listed on the site, so prospective clients may find you. All of your listings and open houses can also be uploaded for viewing by anyone around the world. The NAR's website also allows you to conduct real-time conversations with those who view your listings. By using these resources, you can potentially see a great increase in your business.

## ORGANIZE NETWORKING EFFORTS

Whether you are prospecting for new clients, marketing a property, or interested in learning more about a special type of property from other area agents, it is important to organize your efforts. You will meet many people, and while you might never forget a face, chances are you won't remember enough about each person to be able to successfully initiate another contact. Each part of the three-part networking system described below should be continuous. In other words, you never stop looking for potential contacts, trying to turn potential contacts into active ones, or maintaining your contacts.

✓ **Make a list of potential contacts.** Brainstorm without editing your list, including anyone and everyone mentioned on page 37 in the *Ask for What You Want* section. Then, begin contacting those on your list. Call, or visit their offices or homes and try to meet them in person. Or, you might send a letter of introduction to everyone on your list. Tell them you are now selling real estate, and be certain your marketing identity comes through loud and clear. Don't forget to include a business card.

✓ **Create an active contacts database.** Whenever you get a response to a phone call, visit, or letter, the person who responded becomes an active contact. The difference between potential and active contacts is that you don't know if the potential ones can help you, while active contacts have indicated they may want to buy, sell, refer someone to you, or work with you in some other beneficial way.

To create an active contacts database, begin gathering information about the person who responded. Some agents use software developed specifically for this purpose (see more on technology in Step 3). Others use index cards or pages in a notebook. No matter the method, you will want to be as thorough as possible.

For each contact, note:
    name
    address
    e-mail address
    phone number (work, pager, cell phone, residence)
    fax number
    company name

job title

first meeting—where, when, the topics you discussed

last contact—when, why, and how

✓ **Maintain Your Contacts.** Try to reach people again within a couple of weeks of meeting them. You can send a note of thanks, e-mail a question, or forward a piece of information related to your conversation. This contact cements your meeting in their mind, so they will remember you more readily when you call them again in the future. If you haven't communicated with your contacts for a few months, you might send them a note or e-mail about an article you read, or relevant new technology or law to keep your name fresh in their minds.

## To Review

✓ The skills you need to succeed often are not taught in pre-licensing training. Be open to the fact that you still have much to learn—and the better your skills, the better your chances of meeting, and exceeding, your sales goals.

✓ REALTOR®s who are consistently singled out as top producers agree: there are six personal skills you can't do without. Learn them, and honestly acknowledge which ones you need to work on. Actively pursue improvement in any areas of weakness.

✓ What's the number one Rule of Sales? It's not having the best product, or the best customer service. It's likeability. If your clients don't like you, they won't do business with you. Public interaction skills, therefore, can't be underestimated. Maintain your image as a likeable professional, to buyers, sellers, and other agents at all times.

✓ Marketing yourself is a two-step process. You must first develop a unique marketing identity (some marketing experts refer to this as a branding), and then get that identity in front of potential clients consistently and frequently.

✓ The standard tools for marketing a property—advertisements, signs, listings, open houses—aren't always used to full advantage. Understand and avoid the pitfalls of each to improve results.

✓ The old phrase "time is money" is a reality for agents. You must juggle showing properties; attending previews, closings, office meetings, and listing presentations; working on your own marketing plan; handling paperwork; and many other tasks. Successful agents stay on top of details, and manage their time well. They avoid time wasters such as working with clients who haven't been approved for a mortgage.

✓ Networking is how the top sellers expand their client base; stay on the inside track regarding knowledge of your market; and maintain positive relationships with other agents, lenders, home inspectors, and other professionals they work with. Improve your networking skills, and your business will improve, too.

# USE YOUR COMPUTER LIKE A PRO

WHILE REAL ESTATE IS PRIMARILY KNOWN AS A "PEOPLE BUSINESS," MUCH OF WHAT AGENTS DO TODAY INVOLVES COMPUTERS. OF COURSE, MACHINES AREN'T SUBSTITUTES FOR MEETINGS WITH BUYERS OR SELLERS, BUT THEY CAN LEAD THOSE CLIENTS TO YOU. THEY CAN PUT YOUR LISTINGS IN FRONT OF MILLIONS OF PEOPLE. COMPUTERS MAKE IT EASY FOR YOU TO KEEP IN TOUCH WITH YOUR CLIENT BASE, AND EXPAND IT. THEY ARE ALSO INVALUABLE FOR DOING RESEARCH AND FURTHERING YOUR EDUCATION. IN FACT, YOUR SUCCESS IN REAL ESTATE SALES DEPENDS UPON HOW WELL YOU USE THIS VITAL TOOL.

The use of computers has changed the way realtors do business. While you don't have to become an expert, you will need to be comfortable using the basics. Agents we polled noted that just a few years ago, they carried a heavy MLS book, paper documents, and a key chain. Today, they typically carry a laptop, electronic keys, digital cameras, pagers, and cell phones. They also use the Internet to market themselves and their properties and exchange information with clients and their peers. Don Marcy, an award-winning real estate veteran with over twenty years of sales experience says:

If you're not comfortable with technology today, you might as well find another field. There is no part of this business that lacks some technological aids, and the array of available real estate-related software is mind-boggling. The only real problem is that now, if you take advantage of every possible technological tool and device, you'll need a wheelbarrow to carry them!

---

# ACCESS AND MARKET LISTINGS

The most important reason real estate professionals need a computer is to get their listings noticed, and to view the listings of others. Listings are your inventory, and the computer provides the only access to the Multiple Listing Service (MLS). While the MLS was once a thick book put out every few weeks, it is now an up-to-the-minute resource that includes prices, length of time on the market, pictures, and most of the other details you need to know about a property.

Computers can give hundreds of people access to your listings, even if you don't have a website. There are many local, state, and national websites where you can publicize your properties. Many towns, cities, and counties maintain informational websites that contain real estate listings. They know that new and potential residents look to such sites to learn more about a particular area. Many newspapers will put your listing on their website if you advertise it in print. Hundreds of national sites, such as www.realtor.com and www.realestate.yahoo.com, include listings that are searchable by state, price, and amenities. For more ideas about getting your listings online, use the term "real estate" on any search engine. You'll get links to dozens of sites that can help you promote your properties. When posting your listings online, offer as much information as possible. Home buyers who turn to the Internet to begin their home buying research want details, including the property address, pictures, room sizes, amenities, and landscaping features. If you provide them with the information they want and need, they will be more likely to view the property.

# ORGANIZE WITH SOFTWARE

Many companies have developed computer software specifically targeted to real estate professionals. Your employer is probably already using software to manage his or her business, and may expect you to become familiar with your office's system. But if your brokerage offers limited or no access to computer software, you may want to consider purchasing some for yourself. Virtually every aspect of your business can be computerized, from designing a listing presentation to receiving voice mail.

## Contact Management

Top-selling REALTOR®s have contact lists ranging from hundreds to thousands of people. Keeping track of all of them used to be overwhelming, when agents wrote applicable information on index cards and stored them in a box in their desk. Now, however, you have a wide choice of computer software that you can use to create, update, and manage your list of contacts.

Many contact software programs are called PIMs, or Personal Information Managers. They can be used to organize your time as well as your contacts. Databases that are typically included in professional software packages such as Star Office, Microsoft Office, and WordPerfect Office, can also help you manage your contact list. Word processing programs with mail merge features can create the letters, newsletters, postcards, and brochures you regularly send to your contacts, and then address them all. Many of these programs are free on real estate websites, so make a point of doing some research before making any purchases.

Whatever method you choose, it is to your advantage to manage your list of contacts by using your computer. As you grow in the field, so will your contact list, and your need to keep it organized.

Other types of software programs, all designed to help the real estate professional improve business, include:

real estate forms (print blank or completed forms)
ad writing
calendars and calculators
spell-checkers
contact list managers
lead managers
buyer assistance
website design
direct mailing/marketing/promotional
desktop publishing
financial analysis (qualify buyers)
telemarketing
showings management
prospecting
scheduling
virtual property tours
property management
checkbooks

---

### TECHNOLOGY UPDATE

For its first computerized decade, the MLS was added to and accessed by a few different computer programs. In 1999, the National Association of REALTOR®s approved RETS, or Real Estate Transactions Standards. RETS is a software platform designed to make it easier to exchange of electronic data between different applications. It allows real estate professionals to access and update MLS listings (adding pictures and interactive components) faster and easier than before, no matter what kind of computer they work from.

In addition, many software manufacturers are producing RETS-compliant tools, including a marketing program that allows agents to generate brochures and other promotionals directly from their MLS listings. Other programs schedule property showings live on the Internet, and generate personalized buyer reports that include everything from property information to loan scenarios and school district facts.

---

## BUILD A SUCCESSFUL WEBSITE

More than 68% of all real estate professionals in 2003 had a website, according to a survey conducted by the NAR. Why? Because it is good for business. More than half of all home buyers use the Internet as a source of information, and their numbers are growing. Successful agents are not waiting before they go online to reach them—they're already there.

The good news is that you don't need to be a computer programmer to have your own website. There are hundreds of website creation tools that make the process easy, even for the computer novice. If you use a hosting service, you will probably get a free template you can use to get a simple page or site on the Internet quickly. However, many real estate professionals choose instead to hire someone else to do the job. Why? They cite superior visuals, marketing, and ease of use. They might pay anywhere from a few hundred to a few thousand dollars to designers who often specialize in real estate websites. But when you consider the power of the Internet as a marketing tool, one that you can update as frequently as you like, the cost seems reasonable.

## FIND A HOME, COMPLETE WITH ADDRESS

If you are building your own site, you will first need to secure a domain name, which is your address on the Internet. Most agents choose their own name, or a variation on it (perhaps www.jjsmith.com instead of www.john jaysmith.com). However, you are also free to choose a domain name that represents the marketing identity you established in Step 2. Two examples are www.homesforthemilitary.com or www.propertiesofessex.

---

### HOT TIP

If you have a name that is frequently misspelled, don't buy just one domain name. Purchase the misspellings as well. For example, if your name is Debbie Lang, you should also buy Debby Lang, Debbie Lange, and other misspellings. You don't want a client to miss your site because they have trouble spelling your name. If you own the misspellings, an incorrect typing of your name will still direct the client to your site. Another bonus of purchasing misspellings is that it prevents others from buying them. You don't want to spend time and money on your website only to find out that a site with a name very similar to yours is being visited by your clients, or may be promoting a product or service that you find offensive.

---

In addition to purchasing a domain name, you will have to pay for a hosting site if your employer doesn't provide this benefit. Most Internet service providers (ISPs) offer this service to their customers. If neither of those options works, you can find an independent web host. Typically, such hosts can also secure domain names, design and maintain your site, promote your site, and provide you with e-mail addresses. Check a search engine such as Google using the term "web hosting" to get an idea of available services. Once you have a host and a domain name, you can begin thinking about the various components of your site. What would you like visitors to your site to see? How can you turn them from browsers into buyers? A quick search of other agents' sites will give you some ideas, but here are the most important factors to consider, according to the pros we surveyed.

## INCLUDE VALUABLE CONTENT

If the information on your site isn't important to its visitors, they won't come back. Potential home buyers will be interested in information about your town or city, including its school system(s). Mortgage rates, and the importance of and steps toward pre-qualification are also important. But spend the most time and effort on your listings. Complete, accurate facts and figures, plenty of good pictures, and even virtual tours are the reasons people are coming to your site. Keep them there with great visuals and useful information.

If you have a number of different kinds of listings, or want to attract consumers in various markets, consider creating different sections of your website to appeal to different types of buyers. For example, a page devoted to first-time buyers could include basic information on the buying process, determining how much house they can afford, and addressing their willingness to overlook minor flaws or easily remedied situations (such as dirt and overgrown shrubs). A page for those looking to buy a second home might explain the tax advantages of owning another property, as well as a guide to desirable locations in your area (waterfront, ski resort, mountains, etc.) where these buyers might want to look.

Of course you don't need to stop with your own listings. If you don't have many, or you want to get into another market (investment properties, for example), you can display the listings of other agents. Choose carefully, however. Potential buyers can go to www.realtor.com and other sites if they want to search through thousands of listings. A select group helps you establish your brand, or expand into a new market, without trying to be all things to all people.

## ACT NOW

You know that most of the For Sale by Owner (FSBO)s end up listed by a realtor. Why not give those statistics to the visitors to your website? Explain how you can save them time and money by handling the sale from the start. But don't stop there. List all of the advantages of working with you, including:

✓ I will develop a marketing plan, and cover its costs. Your home will be seen by thousands of potential buyers through the Multiple Listing Service, and will be advertised in newspapers and other media, and through least one open house.

✓ I am experienced, and will support and guide you through each step of the selling or buying process.

✓ I will give you the information you need to completely understand the buying or selling process, so you will have realistic expectations, and not be caught off guard.

✓ The selling price of your home will reflect current sales of comparable properties in your area, and will be established with your input.

✓ I know how to show off your home to its greatest advantage. I can help you enhance curb appeal, resolve storage issues, highlight special features, and otherwise make it more buyer-friendly.

✓ Only pre-screened buyers will see your property. This will eliminate showing to browsers who don't have the true interest or financial ability to purchase your home.

✓ I have excellent negotiation skills. Acting on your behalf, I can reach an agreement with the buyers (or sellers) in accordance with your directions.

## Brand Your Website

With thousands of real estate websites on the Internet, it is essential that you clearly define and communicate the benefits you offer and how your services are different from the competition. The branding of your website should be consistent with all of your other marketing materials, as explained in Step 2. By branding, or emphasizing your uniqueness, you not only differentiate yourself, but provide a comfort level for visitors to your site.

Branding can also be accomplished through use of testimonials. Ask some of your clients to provide a short description of their purchase or sale, as well as their thoughts on the service you provided. Include those testimonials that speak to the qualities that reinforce your brand. For example, if you are emphasizing teamwork as part of your brand, be certain that the quotes you use include that word or speak to that concept. When potential clients read your testimonials, they will get your message through someone else's words and experiences.

## Consider a Partnership

Maintaining a website is time consuming if you do it yourself, and expensive if you pay someone else to do it for you. Some agents resolve this problem by partnering with another business person who has content pertinent to their sites. For example, you might decide to partner with a lender who could provide a guide to getting a mortgage, a calculator to determine how much house a buyer can afford, current interest rates, and an explanation of the different types of loans available. In return for providing current content, your partner would receive free advertising on your site.

## Include Useful Tools

The number one reason home buyers search the Internet is to look at homes for sale. That means a quality photo of every one of your listings should be on your website, and listings should be easily searchable. By including a photo along with standard listing information, you help buyers narrow their search, and eliminate the time you might have spent showing them homes that were never to their liking.

Interactive features are also a must for your website. Why allow hundreds, if not thousands, of potential clients to view your site, and then move on? Ask for their name, address, e-mail address, and telephone number. This information allows you to contact them, instead of hoping that they contact you. You might link the information page to a button on your home page that reads "I want to buy/sell now." After visitors click the button, and input their contact information, it can automatically be sent to you as a message to your cell phone or digital device, or as an e-mail.

Another way to improve usefulness is to connect your site's visitors with needed services. For example, a lender could take online applications for mortgages or pre-qualifying letters, or a home inspector could schedule inspections. Any way to ease or eliminate a step in the process of buying or selling is a win for both you and your clients.

---

### HOT TIP

A webmaster who builds sites for agents urges, "don't cram your website full of useless information and links. You want your website to lead to direct contact with you, so you need to create a need for your site visitors to do so. If you give them free reports, tips on buying and selling, or access to the MLS, why should they bother to contact you? There are already websites, such as www.realtor.com, that do all of that and more. Your website should tell every visitor that you are likeable and accessible, creating an emotional connection that leads to a direct contact."

---

## UPDATE AND IMPROVE YOUR WEBSITE

Websites become obsolete quickly. Properties sell, prices change, interest rates go up and down. If your site isn't updated frequently, it won't be current, and therefore won't be a worthwhile destination for potential buyers and sellers. Whether you designed your site, or paid someone else to, be certain you can make changes from your own computer as often as you need to.

If your site is not getting many visitors, or it gets plenty but no one registers interest, you may need to improve your site. If you are currently online through the use of inexpensive software that created a "cookie cutter" site, it could be time for an upgrade. If you paid thousands of dollars for a truly unique website, you may simply need to reorganize and beef up your content. Is the site easily searchable, or do you lose clients because it's difficult to navigate? Do you have only a handful of listings on your site because you chose to market only your own? Consider adding carefully chosen properties listed by other realtors.

## MARKET YOUR WEBSITE

Once you develop, or pay someone else to develop your website, you need to market it. If no one can find your site, it won't generate any business for you. Marketing your website is a two-step process; the first centers on your own efforts, and the second involves the Internet.

Your website should always be marketed through all of the standard marketing strategies you already employ. That means adding your Internet address (URL) and e-mail address to the contact information on your business cards, stationery, gifts, advertising, client communications, yard signs, direct mail, e-mail signatures, and print ads. Even your listings can advertise your website. Put a box on each one that reads "as featured on www._____.com" (your URL) and "for further information or to schedule a showing, e-mail me at _____ (your e-mail address)."

But what about potential clients who are surfing the Internet without your URL in hand? For those who don't already know you, you must make it easy find your site. One way to do that is by linking your site to other sites. What types of sites should you consider linking to? Think about where consumers might look for agents on the Internet.

Don't bother with huge sites that list thousands of agents. A recent search of www.realtor.com came up with fifty pages just in Chicago! There is no way to differentiate yourself in a group that large. However, a Chicago mortgage company offers a list of agents on its website, and it contains just five. A Chicago news site also links to a handful of area agents. Choose links that provide a reasonable chance of success.

## SEARCH ENGINES

Perhaps the best way to market your site on the Internet is with search engines. You can submit your site to a variety of search engines, such as AltaVista, Google, Yahoo, and Lycos. If they decide to include it in their index, it will be searchable by keywords, titles, and meta tags. The process sounds complicated, but it's really relatively simple. If you are using website software to produce your own site, the software will guide you as to how to add these words. If someone else is designing your site, they will take care of this step for you. But to be certain you get the best results, brainstorm keywords carefully. Keeping your brand, or marketing identity in mind, think of words and phrases that describe your business. If they are strategically placed on your site, a potential customer will be able to find you more easily.

You can also pay a search engine placement specialist to work on your site. This person will not only work on keywords, titles, and meta tags, but will also monitor your site and ensure that it gets top rankings on the search engines you are indexed on. Rankings are vitally important to the visibility of your site. Think of it this way: If a potential buyer is searching with Yahoo, their results might list thousands of realtor websites. Chances are, they will only visit sites in the first few pages of those results. Therefore, the higher your ranking (meaning the closer you are to being on the first page), the more likely your site will get a visit.

Consider a relatively new way to improve rankings: purchasing them. Over a dozen search engines now offer a service, called "pay per click," (or "pay per placement"), which gives you a top position on the results pages, and then charges you every time someone clicks to your site from that search engine. This practice is growing in popularity, evidenced by the number of websites devoted to the practice, and the number of web masters who offer to manage your pay per click (PPC) marketing. You can learn more about PPC on sites such as www.payperclickguide.com and www.payperclickanalyst.com.

---

### MEASURE YOUR SUCCESS

There are a number of ways to measure your marketing success. Most websites can track a variety of numbers that can help determine whether your efforts are being rewarded. The statistics you need to know are:

- ✓ How many hits come from unique first time visitors?
- ✓ How many hits are return visits?
- ✓ Which pages are most popular?
- ✓ If you are linked to other sites, which links refer the most visitors to your site?
- ✓ What is your response rate relative to the number of visitors to your site?
- ✓ How many face-to-face appointments were set through your site?
- ✓ What percentage of customer feedback is positive?

---

# KEEP IN TOUCH:
# THE IMPORTANCE OF E-MAIL

One of the best, and easiest, ways to stay in contact with your client base and form ties with potential clients is with e-mail. Many of your customers and prospects already rely on e-mail, and check their messages several times each day. Using this tool to answer their questions, confirm meetings, and initiate face-to-face meetings is convenient and time-saving. Unlike the telephone, which requires that both parties be available at the same time to have a conversation, e-mail allows you to "converse" with a client when he or she might be busy. In return, they can respond when you are otherwise unavailable.

E-mail is a fast and easy way to develop and deliver documents such as contracts and listings. They can be attached easily to your message, and then downloaded and printed by the recipient. You can also send electronic newsletters, complete with pictures, that keeps your name fresh in the minds of your contact list. You might send market updates to those who've done business with you in the past, send new listings to clients who are thinking of buying, or introduce yourself and offer your services to a group of potential buyers or sellers.

However, the convenience of e-mailing can also be its downside. Because it's quick and easy, and often used to send messages to family and friends, it doesn't always feel like business. Professional e-mailing has rules, which, if not followed, can lead to a "casual" trap that diminishes the effectiveness of this communication tool. In other words, treat e-mail the way you would any other business correspondence. Follow these guidelines to ensure successful e-mailing:

1.  **Practice netiquette.** Online etiquette doesn't differ from other business protocol. Manners count! Thank every customer who e-mails you. Maintain a courteous and professional tone. If a prospect has initiated contact online, respond in kind. They expect an e-mail, not a phone call or a letter.

2.  **Make use of your mail program's capabilities.** Grammar and spelling count, so proofread and use spell check before sending any e-mail. Use only the regular font style (avoid bold, italics, and all caps); other styles can look unprofessional, and are not readable by all mail programs. Set up a signature file that will automatically attach itself to the end of every e-mail you send. It should include all of your contact information, including URL, and, if you have one, a marketing identity phrase.

3.  **Respond promptly.** Check and respond to your e-mail at least three times a day. Your clients and prospects expect prompt attention, and this is typically how often they check their e-mail. If you are away from your computer, you can use an autoresponder to send a generic reply

immediately (see the discussion below for more ideas about how to use autoresponders). Another way to keep up with e-mail while away from your computer is to invest in a wireless e-mail system. For an initial charge and monthly fee, you can access e-mail through a cell-phone-type device with a small keyboard no matter where you are.

---

### TECHNOLOGY UPDATE

Autoresponders are great for getting to clients and prospects immediately, promising them that they will receive a personal response within a specified period of time. But autoresponders can do even more for your business. If you are frustrated by the low number of face-to-face meetings you schedule with the hundreds of people who visit your website, an autoresponder can help.

The key to getting leads from e-mails and website visitors is to offer specific, useful information that addresses a need they specified when writing to you or visiting your site. Did they say they are thinking of buying? Send an e-mail offering a "mini course" on how to get through the process. If they indicated they want to buy, send an e-mail with information on a small group of local lenders who can help them get a pre-qualifying letter. By tailoring your response to their needs, you begin to form a relationship without lifting a finger, or your phone receiver.

The contact process can consist of one exchange, or many. "Smart" autoresponders can be programmed to send successive e-mails at intervals you specify. For example, a visitor to your website indicated that he or she is relocating to your area. Your autoresponder can immediately send an e-mail with valuable information about relocating. Then, it can send another e-mail asking if they received the information, and letting them know you are available to help them. If you don't hear from them, the autoresponder can send a third e-mail later that day, or the next day, with even more relocation information. You have just made three "personal" contacts with this prospect without any effort! When you call them for the first time, a connection already exists, making your job easier.

# USE E-MAIL FOR MARKETING

Compare the traditional mailing of a postcard or letter with sending an e-mail. The traditional mailing costs hundreds of dollars in materials and postage, while the e-mail is virtually free. Traditional mailings take time to organize and disburse, while any number of e-mails are prepared just once, and sent with the click of button. It is no wonder successful real estate agents are turning to their computers to do their marketing.

## DEVELOP A DATABASE

The first step in marketing with e-mail is developing a database of e-mail addresses. While before you collected street addresses for mailings, now concentrate on collecting e-mail addresses. Ask for the e-mail address of every buyer or seller you worked with in the past. When someone sends you an e-mail, add his or her name to your address book. To keep that contact information up to date, dedicate two hours a month to going through the database, updating the information on the existing entries, and adding any new ones.

### HOT TIP

Just as there are companies that sell lists of telephone numbers and street addresses, there are ones that sell lists of e-mail addresses. First thought? An easy way to fill up your database. However, the agents we polled insist, "don't waste your money!" Mass mailing, whether of e-mails or print material, typically get a positive response rate of less than 1%. While people are used to "junk mail," and are willing to toss whatever they don't find to be of immediate use, they are less forgiving of unwanted e-mails, especially if that e-mail was generated by someone in their community. There is no point in alienating thousands of people in the hopes of making a handful of sales.

## TARGET YOUR MAILINGS

You can set up e-mail groups by category to target mailings. For example, create one group for first-time home buyers and another for second-home candidates. Or, add groups of real estate agents, previous clients, and traditional geographic farm-out areas. Another group could be formed of those who have visited your website. The more specific your group, the better you can tailor your marketing content to each.

## VIRTUAL TOURS

After you acquire a listing, create a virtual tour of the property. Put the tour on your website, and send an e-mail to all of the agents in your database. The e-mail should include a link to the tour page of your website. You could also simply e-mail the tour, however getting agents to visit your site means they might find another listing that could be of interest to one of their buyers. This technique has worked well for hundreds of agents, who report that they often get a sale before the property makes it into the MLS.

## NEWSLETTERS

Many agents develop newsletters that are e-mailed regularly to everyone in their database. You could also post the newsletter on your website, and e-mail a link to it. Include anything that might be of interest, but avoid filling it with useless information. The newsletter should serve as a way of keeping in touch. Because you are sending the newsletter to a varied audience (prospects, previous clients, agents, etc.) do not use specifically targeted information. However, even the general nature of the content should convey your personality or brand.

## SPECIFIC MAILINGS

When using targeted groups, include content that they can use. Marketing statistics, listing activities, and neighborhood or community information are all good content. Make the e-mail look personal, rather than like a form letter. Your database software should allow you to include the name of the recipient, rather than the entire list of recipients, on each e-mail. Be sure to give every recipient the opportunity to "opt out" if they don't want to receive further e-mails. Add a link at the bottom of your message that contacts you so that you can remove their name from your list.

A great advantage to specific e-mailings is that they can be forwarded easily, spreading your message to even more people. Can you imagine a client saving a postcard and passing it on to a friend? Probably not. But an e-mail with good information can be forwarded with a few mouse clicks.

# STAY INFORMED: RESEARCH AND EDUCATION

Technological advances, especially those pertaining to the Internet, have made it easier than ever before to keep your skills sharp, and keep up with market changes and trends. When you know where to find the research and education sites you need, you can take advantage of them, and increase your sales success on your own time, in your own home.

## KNOW THE COMPETITION

On the Internet, you can browse through thousands of real estate sites, such as those set up by national agencies, local brokerages, and individual agents. You can see listings, and get marketing ideas from other agents. As a visitor to someone else's site, you get a unique vantage point that can help you make positive changes to your own site. What is effective in the sites you visit? What bores you, or causes you to click away to another site? Use your browsing as an opportunity to learn from others' achievements and mistakes.

In addition, you can visit or join groups of agents who gather on the Internet to share helpful tips and techniques for success. Ask a question, or simply search and read through the message archives to find useful information. To find such groups, review the section in Step 2 regarding Online Discussion Groups, found on page 38.

## FURTHER YOUR EDUCATION

You can get information, brush up on your facts, and even take classes, on many subjects pertinent to the field of real estate on the Internet. Here is a sampling of categories of interest:

✓ **News and Trends**
   Many real estate sites offer news, market analysis, and reports on current trends. This type of information is vital to your business, and you will want to visit the sites often for updates. There won't be time to look at all of the hundreds of sites regularly, but before narrowing down, check out as many of them as you can. Use the suggestions below, or conduct a search using the terms "real estate," "news," and "trends." Depending on the area in which you live and work, you may find sites that are specifically geared toward your market.

   After you've found a few sites that provide the news and information you can use, bookmark them on your Internet browser, and build time into your schedule to perform this kind of research at least once a week. You can use the information you gather in electronic newsletters, mailings to your client list, and even in listing presentations. Your image as a professional will be enhanced as you impart timely, relevant facts and figures.

---

### WEB SITES WITH REAL ESTATE
### NEWS AND ANALYSIS

| | |
|---|---|
| **www.reis.com** | This free site has real estate news and analysis, but Reis also offers a subscriber edition (Reis SE) with more market information and analytical tools. |
| **www.realestatejournal.com** | Published by the *Wall Street Journal*, this site contains news, mortgage rate information, and loan calculators. |
| **www.realtor.org** | The website of the National Association of REALTOR®s has news, education, business tools (such as a marketing guide), survey results, and an online university. Full site access requires membership and registration. |
| **www.realtytimes.com** | Offers a daily market conditions report, marketing and technology advice, a monthly newsletter, and a custom newsfeed which can be purchased for inclusion on your website or printed marketing materials. |
| **www.inman.com** | Inman News bills itself as the nation's leading independent real estate news service and content provider to the real estate industry. News is presented by category, including technology, mortgage, and brokerage. Unique features include its "rookie real- |

tor" and blog sections. It costs
$149.95/year for complete
access.

www.ired.com        International Real Estate Digest
has an "Agent's Toolkit" that
includes information on marketing, calculators, agent support
services, and a shop where you
can order books, signs, and
software.

www.hud.gov         The federal government's
Department of Housing and
Urban Development offer statistics and reports on homeowner-
ship, policy and legislation, and
fair housing issues.

---

## ✓ Home Styles and Construction Terms

When showing properties, you know the importance of being
knowledgeable about architecture and home construction. While
some of this information was probably covered in your pre-licensing
training, you may find that you are confronting styles and equipment
about which you know very little. For instance, do you know the difference between a gambrel roof and a hip roof? Can you explain the
benefits of a high R-value to your clients?

The easiest way to brush up on this knowledge is to first create a list
of the problems you have encountered in this area. Were many of the
listings in your market built in the Victorian period? Are homes in your
area affected by radon, lead paint, or mold? Research the information
you need by being as specific as possible. Sites such as http://
faculty.ccc.edu/khope/hum202architlex.html offer glossaries of terms,
while others present pictures and descriptions. On www.usinspect
.com's glossary of terms is linked to a picture of a house. You simply
click on the area of the house to get a definition. Its "House Facts"

section has information on components and systems ranging from air conditioning to woodstoves; household pests; and environmental concerns. With websites such as these available, there is no excuse for not knowing, for example, the difference between a casement and a double-hung window.

✓ **Courses and Educational Software**

There are online courses offered in every subject imaginable. Many states accept continuing education credits earned online, and there are numerous designations and certifications offered through distance education. The National Association of REALTOR®s has its own online university, with classes in subjects such as International Real Estate; Mold, Lead, and Radon; and Negotiating.

General online education sites also offer courses in real estate-related topics, and more universal business subjects that could be of interest to agents. On www.WorldWideLearn.com, a directory of programs from dozens of distance learning centers, there are courses in continuing education topics such as sales, marketing, and time management. For more ideas about online education, search the Internet with the terms "real estate" and "online education."

Educational software can perform the same function as online courses. You can proceed through and absorb information at your own pace, at home or in the office. However, the cost is typically lower, and, since you own the software, you can review the material covered at any time. In addition to licensing exam preparation, you can find software that helps develop specific business skills, as well as software that helps run your business more smoothly. Sites offering real estate software include:

| | |
|---|---|
| **Realty Guide** | www.xmission.com/~realtor1/software.htm #SOFT |
| **Realty Star** | www.realtystar.com/index.html |
| **Real Estate Center** | recenter.tamu.edu/soft/ |
| **Z-law** | www.z-law.com/ |

## To Review

✓ Your computer is the most powerful tool you can use to achieve sales success. The more adept you are with it, the better it will serve you.

✓ Access the Multiple Listing Service (MLS) online for the most current listing information.

✓ Get your listings online even if you don't have a website and offer them to local, regional, and state sites, as well as real estate-related sites.

✓ Use software to organize your business. It will save you time, and make it easy to contact your client list, prospect, prepare listing presentations, keep track of visitors to your website, and more.

✓ Whether you design it yourself, or pay a professional to do it for you, go online with your own website.

✓ Include content that will be valuable to your site's visitors, and update it often.

✓ Brand your website to stand out from the crowd and introduce yourself positively to hundreds of prospective buyers and sellers.

✓ Make your website interactive. Ask for visitors' contact information, and ask them to identify themselves as a buyer, seller, or browser. Offer online help in the form of pre-qualifying, scheduling a home inspection, or requesting a market analysis.

✓ Market your website by including your URL (Internet address) on business cards, brochures, signs, and every other printed marketing piece you distribute. Create a signature line for e-mails that also includes your URL.

✓ Get your website indexed on search engines for maximum visibility. Consider hiring a professional to improve your rankings, and investigate the "pay per click" services offered on many search engines.

✓ Use e-mail to keep in touch with your contact list. Remember to treat e-mail as you would any other business correspondence.

✔ Consider using an autoresponder to help with e-mailing.

✔ To market yourself with e-mails, first develop a database of contacts' e-mail addresses. You can send targeted mailings to specific groups within your database, and send more general newsletters regularly to everyone else in your database.

✔ Use the Internet to stay informed. Investigate competitors' websites to see what works, and what doesn't. Keep abreast of news and trends by frequently visiting real estate news sites. Research topics you need to learn more about, such as construction terms and architectural styles.

✔ Online courses and educational software can save you time and money. Some states recognize continuing education credits earned online, and many designations and certificates can be acquired online, too. More general skills such as sales and marketing can be improved through courses and educational software.

# MEET THE NEEDS OF BUYERS AND SELLERS

THERE ARE TWO SIDES TO EVERY REAL ESTATE TRANS-
ACTION, AND YOU WILL BE ON EACH ONE HUNDREDS OF
TIMES DURING YOUR CAREER. MANY OF THE SKILLS
NEEDED TO WORK EFFECTIVELY WITH BUYERS AND
SELLERS ARE THE SAME; HOWEVER, THERE ARE ALSO
SPECIFIC APPROACHES THAT CAN HELP YOU BEST
WORK A DEAL FOR ONE SIDE OR THE OTHER. UNDER-
STANDING THE DIFFERENCES BETWEEN REPRESENT-
ING A BUYER AND SELLER IS A HALLMARK OF THE
SUCCESSFUL AGENT.

Most real estate buyers have been sellers before, and obviously sellers have previously purchased properties. So you might think they understand both sides of the transaction. Wrong! Prior experience probably won't translate into working knowledge. In other words, don't assume that a buyer or seller will know how a sale will proceed. It is your job to educate them. Each side will require different approaches and information. Tell them everything they need to know about the real estate process. Education not only creates great agents; it creates great buyers and sellers, too.

## DEALING WITH BUYERS

Buyers are considered by some successful agents to be easier to work for than sellers. To begin with, they come to you asking for your services. As soon as they are pre-qualified for a mortgage, and explain what they are looking for, you can begin showing them homes. Consider, on the other hand, that you will probably need to work to find sellers. When you find them, there is a multiple-step process which must take place before you can list their properties. Developing listing presentations, taking and uploading digital pictures and virtual tours, and creating a marketing plan take time.

In addition to the fact that buyers bring commission checks with less work for you, there is great satisfaction to be found in helping someone find the right property. Don and Bert Marcy, agents from New Jersey who have made the list of the state's top salespeople for over 20 years, note that they enjoy "playing matchmaker. The real thrill is finding the right fit. You need to have the ability to understand what people are really looking for. Then, you go out and work like crazy to help them find it."

## HANDLING FIRST-TIME BUYERS

Some first-time buyers act like old pros. They know what they want, understand what they can afford, and keep an open mind when you're showing them properties. Most, however, are more challenging. Buying a home is an enormous investment, and with the large price tag can come a large amount of nervousness.

When dealing with jittery buyers, keep in mind that nerves are related to a fear of the unknown, which is best mitigated with information. The more information you give them, the less they'll worry. By keeping such buyers "in the loop," you will minimize their jitters, which will in turn minimize the number of anxious phone calls they make to you!

Throughout the buying process, explain each step thoroughly. In particular, it is critical for the buyers to understand:

1.  why they need to be pre-qualified

2.  what purchase documents look like (give them samples that they can take to their attorney or review on their own)

3. how the offer process works (e.g., when their offer is accepted, they are obligated to purchase)

4. what happens if there is already an offer on a property they want to buy, or if another buyer makes an offer after they have made one

5. how you handle their earnest money deposit (the procedure varies by state, and deposits are not always returned if the deal falls through)

---

### ACT NOW

Even if you don't have a buyer yet, make up a calendar form that you can use to help them through the process. The form should reflect your market identity or brand, and contain all of your contact information, including URL. List all of the steps in the buying process, personalized information (you can add the buyers' names at the top with a heading such as "The Smith's Home Purchase Calendar"), and the dates on which contingencies expire.

---

## WORKING WITH INTERNET-SAVVY BUYERS

More than half of all buyers use the Internet to search for homes before they contact an agent. California REALTOR® Donna Dawson says there are real advantages to working with these buyers. "They have a better sense of what the market is like; there are fewer surprises and cases of 'sticker shock.' Since they're constantly surfing the Internet for listings, they expect me to also, and that keeps me on my toes."

There are downsides of working with such active buyers, though. Many of the commercial listing sites aren't updated frequently. Eager buyers will find homes that interest them, and contact you with addresses or MLS numbers to arrange showings, only to find out that the properties have already been sold. But this downside gives you an opportunity to explain a benefit of using your services: you have the most current listing information, and can therefore more easily find the type of home they are looking for.

Another potential downside is the tendency for Internet-savvy buyers to question your commission. They might not directly ask you to lower it, but they could ask you to justify it. Be prepared to explain why the services you offer are worth the price. Let them know you are an experienced professional; you have been through the process many times, and know how to deal with sellers, other agents, lenders, appraisers, and inspectors. Your expertise will make the sale go more smoothly, with an outcome they will appreciate.

Come up with a specific plan to deal with the commission-cutting question. Veteran agent Nancy Lang cautions, "it might make sense to cut your commission if a deal is close, and everyone else is giving a little. But don't make it a habit. It can undermine your standing as a professional. If you don't respect your profession, why should anyone else?" Whatever you decide, don't waffle, and don't get emotional. It's nothing personal.

Once you've closed with Internet-savvy clients, maintain contact through e-mail. Share useful information, such as details of cost-effective home improvements, updates on local zoning laws, and tips on how to maximize the value of their property. These buyers will forward e-mails when they contain something of value. When they pass on one of your messages, they've helped you expand your sphere of influence with no effort on your part.

## SHOULD YOU BECOME A BUYER'S REPRESENTATIVE?

Until recently, all agents worked for the seller. The listing agent had the most direct involvement, but everyone who showed the property, and the agent who sold it, were known as sub-agents. Instead of holding the buyers' interests above those of the seller, the sub-agent would, in fact, favor the seller.

Many buyers are asked to sign a statement acknowledging that they understand this practice.

Understandably, consumers put pressure on the real estate industry to change the practice of sub-agency. The industry responded with education, designations, and a change of climate to help agents more fairly represent the buyer in real estate transactions. In 1988, The Real Estate Buyer's Agent Council (REBAC) was founded to promote the skills and services of buyers' agents. REBAC now has over 40,000 members, and awards a professional designation to those who meet course requirements and have the requisite professional experience. The Accredited Buyer Representative (ABR) designation is the only one of its type recognized by NAR.

According to REBAC, buyers who use an ABR find homes sooner and on average are shown three more properties than those who work with traditional agents. That explains why over half of all buyers choose an ABR. Why should you consider attaining this designation and becoming a buyer's agent? To begin with, it can help you carve out a niche within a very competitive market. It's a numbers game: the 63% of buyers who use an ABR don't have many to choose from. Of the more than 2.1 million people licensed to sell real estate in the United States, less than 5% are designated buyers' agents.

When you represent the buyer, you focus on just one side of the transaction. That means you can save time and money by being able to market your services to one specific group. Buyers' agents target their promotions, including print materials, website and other Internet presence, and business cards and stationary, to appeal only to buyers. You can also offer more to your clients. Beyond the traditional MLS, you can present to your buyers FSBOs, foreclosures, and other properties not listed by your fellow agents.

ABRs are not directly competing with listing agents, who need their services to help sell homes. Listing agents therefore frequently give referrals to ABRs. Working as a buyers' agent can get you on the inside track with these agents more quickly than if you worked with both buyers and sellers.

If you are considering becoming a buyers' agent, research the subject of dual agency and the laws of your state. Current legislation in many areas of the country is challenging the practice of one brokerage using two agents to represent the two sides of a transaction. If the practice of dual agency becomes illegal in your state, as an ABR you will be poised to grab a good share of the buyers' market.

---

### CHECKING NEGATIVITY

What is the biggest misstep you can make with a buyer? Allowing negativity to creep into your conversations. Any type of criticism, whether it be directed at a property, a neighborhood, or another agent, can erode buyer confidence. Don't assume that you know enough about your buyer to be able to read his or her mind. Buyers hire you to show them the possibilities, not to weed out certain types of homes or streets for them.

If you are working with a buyer who can't make a decision, your negativity, however well you think you guard it, could be to blame. Instead of disapproval, show each property with an eye toward its possibilities. Every home has them, whether they be price, condition and/or location. When you check your negativity at the door, you are more likely to help the buyer find the home they've been looking for.

---

## INTERVIEWING THE BUYER

Before you begin showing properties, there are two critical actions you must take with any buyer. Prequalification is first. To refresh your memory, refer back to page 29 in Step 2 for a script that can be used to lead buyers toward pre-qualification. The second action is the interview. Don't assume that you can read your buyer's mind, or even that what he or she first tells you they want in a home is what they'll end up buying. Conducting a thorough interview, in which you listen far more than you speak, is the key to helping buyers find the right properties.

Begin your interview with a discussion about price. Using the pre-qualification letter, help the buyer determine what can be afforded. There may be some room to negotiate, so listen carefully to what is being said. Is there an indication that the "perfect" home could bring the buyer to spend a little more? Or is strict adherence to a budget very important?

Next, ask questions, pausing to listen carefully to the answers. Take good notes. Many agents put these questions on a form, with space for each one to be rated as a need or want, or ranked in importance from one (most important) to five (least important). Don't give the form to your buyer(s), but instead use it to make notes during the interview.

Typical buyers' interview questions include:

How many bathrooms and bedrooms do you need?
Is there a particular style home you prefer/dislike?
What amount of square footage do you like or need?
Are you willing to look at homes that need some renovating?
Describe your dream bathroom/kitchen.
Are there any access issues, such as members of the family who can't
   negotiate stairs?
How important is the quality of the school system?
What else would you like: fireplace, garage, basement (finished?),
   family room?

During the interview, explain the importance of flexibility. Many homes in the MLS are overpriced, not well maintained, in a poor location, or have some other defect. If buyers' expectations are realistic, and they understand that perfection is a rarity, the process will go more smoothly. Remind buyers that if you help them find a great deal, they can always add those items that are missing from their "need" list, or make updates or improvements to turn an average home into a dream home. Managing their expectations before you start showing them properties is essential.

## SHOWING PROPERTIES

Top-seller Brenda Eager points out the importance of selecting properties carefully, using the notes you took during the buyer interview. "Don't send them out with 100 listings. It's overwhelming, and doesn't look like you put much thought into it. Select just three properties at a time, and encourage your buyers to take notes during the viewing."

It's also important to continue the interview process as you look at properties together. To get the best feedback, ask open-ended questions, and keep your opinions to yourself. It is your job to bring the inventory to the customer, not to decide for him or her what best suits them. You might want to encourage them to "rate" each property by using "plus" and "minus" columns. For some buyers, seeing the home in black and white terms can help when it's time to make a decision. If the price, location, and total square footage are in the plus column, and lack of a wood-burning fireplace is in the minus column, you could point out how close the property is to what they want.

---

### ACT NOW

Take the advice of Michigan agent Brenda Eager. Order dozens of plastic clipboards and pens imprinted with your name and contact information. When showing properties, give them to your buyer with the listing printouts attached. Encourage them to take notes directly on the listings, and to bring the whole clipboard home. Instead of getting confused hours later about which house had the pool and which one needed a new bathroom, they can refer directly to their notes. Plus, your name and number are on every sheet of paper, the pen, and the clipboard!

---

## DEALING WITH A BUYER'S SPECIAL NEEDS

Some of your buyers may be facing difficult situations that necessitate their move. You need to treat them differently from other buyers, while keeping in mind that they still want the same outcome: to purchase a home. If a buyer is going through a divorce, facing foreclosure, or being relocated reluctantly, their needs will vary from those of the typical buyer. Helping them to understand what's available while not rushing them to make a decision, is critical for success with this type of buyer.

During the interview, listen carefully without judging. You don't need to offer an opinion about the lousy company, husband, wife, bank, lawyer, etc. Determine what will make this buyer feel that his or her needs are met. Are they worried about security? Did they love their old neighborhood and now hope to find that same sense of camaraderie in a new one? Do they have worries about money? Each situation calls for a different approach. It's your job to give or lead them to not only the right property, but to the right information that can help meet their needs.

For example, if your buyers are worried about safety, first find out as much as you can about the area they are moving from. Use this information to favorably compare and contrast your area with the old location. Gather crime statistics for your area to show that the crime rate is low. Find properties with strong neighborhood associations and neighborhood watch programs. If you are working with a buyer who has financial concerns, you need to show them that they can afford the properties you are showing them. Cost-of-living and mortgage calculators give accurate pictures of what can be expected. If the buyer knows they can meet the new payments, their concerns will be alleviated. When dealing with buyers with special needs, it is important to remember that you are a REALTOR®. That might seem simple, but people going through difficult times are apt to share more sensitive emotional information than they would at other times. You are not a social worker or a psychologist. Listen, show empathy, but remember why you were hired. If you can help them find the right property, you will have taken one of their problems off the list.

# ALL ABOUT SELLERS

Sellers keep everyone in the field of real estate solvent. They pay the commission that is split between their agent and the buyer's agent. Therefore, even if you are a buyers' agent, the seller indirectly controls your income. However, the seller doesn't always make it that simple. Most homeowners feel a sense of attachment to their homes; perhaps their child was married in the backyard, or they renovated the kitchen together. Life happens at home, and for some sellers, it's not easy parting. Understanding what motivates the seller, and how best to work with him or her, will make the process easier, as well as rewarding, both financially and personally.

## PRESENTING AND PREPARING A LISTING

Working with a seller starts with an initial meeting. Whether it takes place in person or over the phone, this meeting is when you will gather as much information about the seller and the property as possible. The seller may be interviewing a number of other agents, which means you will have to compete for the listing. If this is the case, the presentation you put together based on the information you gathered in the initial meeting will either win or lose the business for you.

Jill Birdsall, an agent in Albany County, New York, urges "find out what the seller wants. Don't assume it is getting top dollar for their property. If you ask open-ended questions, and really listen to the answers, you can get them talking. Since sellers aren't typically as open as buyers, that's important. For some sellers, a quick closing is what they're after, and others are willing to wait for the right offer."

The easiest way to assure that you ask all the right questions, and don't leave anything out, is to prepare a form for interviewing sellers. Type it and print out multiple copies. Every time you speak with or meet with a new seller, fill it out. You will have an accurate record of your discussion, and a document that will make it easy for you prepare a listing presentation. A seller meeting form might look like this:

Property _____ Date _____

Seller's Name and Address _____

Phone (home/cell) _____ Fax _____

E-mail address _____

Why are you selling your property? _____

When do you need to sell? _____

At what price would you like to list your home? _____

Tell me about your home: type _____

square footage _____

# bedrooms _____

bathrooms _____

other amenities _____

How did you hear about me/my agency? _____

_____

Are you interviewing other agents? If yes, who are they, and when are

they making their presentations? _____

What criteria are you using to select an agent? _____

Would you prefer to meet in your home, or at my office? _____

When I make my listing presentation, can all the sellers be present?

_____

Would you be willing to wait to make a decision as to who will be your

agent until I can meet with you? _____

After you conduct the initial interview, you need to gather even more information. Research the neighborhood if you're not familiar with it. What have similar homes in that area sold for? You will need this data to perform a Comparable Market Analysis (CMA). But don't stop your research with comparables that have been sold. Also look at market activity for comparables in actives, under contract, pending, withdrawn, and expireds. In addition, find out when the sellers bought the property, and for what price.

Drive by the home, and all of the comparable properties you researched, and take digital photos. Assess the positives and negatives of the property in writing. Rate the curb appeal, location, quality compared to other homes on the street, paint job, and landscaping.

At the listing presentation, this thorough preparation will show, and thus enhance your professional image. You want the seller to begin to trust and have confidence in you from the start, so begin by showing them that you took the time to know everything you could about their home and its location.

During the actual presentation, use body language to your advantage. Firm handshakes, eye contact, and an open posture (no crossed arms or slouching) all inspire confidence. If you are using presentation software, be sure that you can control the speed at which the presentation unfolds. Break often from the computer to speak directly to the seller. The focus should be on you, and not your laptop.

---

### KEEP IN MIND

Presentation software and a computer to run it on are expensive. But so is giving away all of your research and marketing ideas. If you leave printed material with the seller, and he or she chooses not to list with you, you've given them hours of work that they, and their agent, can use free of charge. Consider computer or Internet presentations not only because they are state-of-the-art and attention-grabbing, but also because they protect your work.

---

If you do work from print, make it stand out. Use color pages, and bind the presentation. The cover should be personalized ("Especially Prepared for . . .") and include a photo of the home. Customize the picture with an effect such as soft crop, custom frame, and/or drop shadow. You may use software specifically designed to generate listing presentation materials, such as IMPREV or Hewlett Packard Real Estate, or use a word processing program such as Microsoft Word or Publisher.

Whether working from a computer or print material, there is set ground that needs to be covered. Each element of your presentation works toward the same goal: getting the seller to have confidence that your services will sell his or her home not only better that he or she could themselves, but better than any other agent. These elements include:

✓ a cover letter that introduces you and describes your experience. Include statistics from your website, such as number of hits and site placement, as well as your sales history.

✓ your resume, which lists all designations, awards, and achievements.

✓ an overview of your company, including all sellers' benefits.

✓ a description of the property including taxes, sales history, and current mortgage.

✓ a personalized CMA with photos and descriptions (including days on the market) of competing active, under contract, withdrawn, and expired homes.

✓ a pricing chart that offers a range of prices (never specify an exact price), and which is clearly based on the CMA.

✓ testimonials from former clients.

✓ a comprehensive marketing plan to sell the home including print (flyers, brochures, postcards) media (newspaper, TV, and/or radio), virtual tours, and the Internet (your website, the MLS, and any other sites you plan to use).

✓ all listing forms, completed to the degree possible, including a listing agreement.

✓ tips on preparing the property for sale, including staging advice.

As you go through your presentation, the seller will be listening for a short list of things: price, commission, marketing strategy, and expected timeframe for a sale. The agents we surveyed offered some great advice for dealing with both price and commission issues. Before giving the seller a price range, and after you've presented the CMA, ask them what they think their home should sell for. If they can't come up with a number, give them your price range, explaining how it was determined. Then, complete a net sheet that already includes the property information and your commission. If working from a range, use an average of the highest and lowest prices.

By not addressing the commission directly, you lead the discussion in your favor. Talk about it in terms of their net proceeds. It's simply one line item in a list of costs associated with selling a home. If the seller turns the discussion to commission cutting, be prepared with a rehearsed answer (refer back to the section on the Internet-Savvy Buyers on page 69). Include the strength of your marketing plan as part of your answer. Emphasize that the plan you've come up with is not only unique, but the product of experience and training. Susan Sommers, a consistent multi-million-dollar producer who specializes in first-time sellers emphasizes: "educate the seller up front. Explain the many complicated steps it takes to sell a home, and how you will guide them through every one. If they understand what your services are, they will understand the commission."

---

### HOT TIP

Consider putting a virtual tour online a week before the property will be listed. You can generate many calls from interested buyers, who will be directed to an open house the next week. The open house will be well-attended, and you will have created an environment similar to an auction. The buyers will already be familiar with, and interested in, the home. They'll know they are in competition with one another if they choose to make an offer.

---

When you give a well-prepared listing presentation, you exude confidence. All of your research puts you in a position in which there is no question you can't answer. Every number and statistic you cite is accurate and defendable. With this confidence, address the seller who is interviewing other agents by asking if you can come back after all the other presentations have been given.

---

### SHOULD YOU TAKE THE LISTING?

New agents are hungry for business, and often take whatever they can get. But is every listing worth your time, money, and energy? Here are a few situations in which it could be best to walk away:

- You would never consider buying the property, or showing it to friends and relatives.
- The home shows poorly, and the seller doesn't want to spend any money improving it.
- The seller's price and/or timeframe expectations are unreasonable.
- The home has structural problems, which the seller will not address prior to listing.
- The seller won't agree to your commission rate and terms.

---

Congratulations! The seller has agreed to list with you. At this time, take out the prepared listing agreement, and fill in the price. Refer to this number as the amount you all agree on. Wait for an affirmative response before moving on. Then, explain that in order to write a listing that will motivate buyers to take a look, you will need more information. Take accurate measurements and interior digital photos. Find out what appliances and fixtures stay with the house, and what the seller plans to remove. This is a detail often overlooked by anxious agents, which can cause problems later. Ask any other questions which will help you write a great listing.

## Pricing Strategies

Your goal in listing a home is to get the right buyer through the door, quickly. Price every property with that goal in mind. If the figure is too high, you severely limit the number of buyers who will even consider the home. Too low, and you find yourself in the position of dealing with an angry seller who can't net the amount they need.

If you haven't worked with many buyers, enlist the help of a more experienced agent to determine the price "cut-offs" for your area. Typical buyers might ask to see homes in the $100,000 to $150,000 range in one city, and $99,000 to $149,000 in another. Whatever upper limit your price is higher than, consider dropping it to fall within that lower range. For example, if you are thinking of listing at $155,000, and a typical search is for homes in the $125,000 to $150,000 range, remember that just $5,000 less will make your listing appear in the searches of many more buyers.

To emphasize this point with sellers, perform a number of MLS searches on your laptop in front of them. Show them how many homes fall into each search category. If they see for themselves that pricing a few thousand dollars less will place them in the search results of many more buyers, they are more likely to understand your pricing strategy. But remember that they must ultimately set the price. You are there to educate and guide, not to coerce.

Jill Birdsall, an agent from Albany County, New York, notes: "pricing is not an exact science. Do your homework, know the neighborhood, the comparables, and the property for sale. But the seller has the ultimate authority." How should you deal with a seller who insists on an unrealistically high price? Calmly explain the advantages of setting one that's more competitive:

1. More buyers will be introduced to your home.

2. The right price often means less negotiation.

3. Agents prefer to show well-priced homes.

4. You are more likely to get offers, and a sale, in a shorter period of time.

What if a seller mentions another agent who cited a higher listing price? First, remind them of your marketing and pricing goal: to get the most qualified buyers to see the property. Overpricing won't do that. If the higher price is "justified" as negotiating room, ask who will be doing the negotiating? Not a group of buyers pitted against one another, but typically a lone buyer who will expect you to move down to a price such as the one you suggested in the first place. And that lone buyer will probably come along months, not days or weeks, from now.

Explain that length of time on the market can greatly influence sale price. The first few weeks of a listing are typically the most active. After that, showings drop off. When a home sits on the market for a few months, buyers begin to wonder what is wrong with it. Buyers' agents respond by suggesting lower offers. If a property is priced right initially, they can take advantage of the volume of showings, and sell faster at a higher price.

Pricing strategies must also take into account the condition of the house. Some agents are squeamish about bringing up overgrown plantings, odors, and other maintenance issues, but they are doing themselves, and their sellers a disservice if they don't address these problems early in the process. There are two reasons to tactfully discuss the property's obvious negatives. First, there are many easily remedied issues that could cause the house to sit on the market. If the homeowner understands the importance of painting, cleaning, or planting, he or she can take care of these problems prior to listing.

Second, it is a good idea to prepare the seller for the inspection. Don't wait until there is an offer on the house to tell your client you noticed the worn roof a month ago, but thought the inspector might not make an issue of it. Point out every possible problem that an inspector could flag. Give advice on dealing with them, explaining the pros and cons of acting now instead of later. If the seller decides not to make repairs, and they understand that it will affect the sale price, don't be alarmed. Susan Sommers notes that she has sold properties in every kind of condition. "It's not my job to get my sellers to fix up their homes before listing them. It's my job to be professional and knowledgeable. There is no 'one size fits all' approach, no one right or wrong way to sell property."

If the seller is unrealistic about pricing (demanding a high price and expecting a quick sale at that price), suggest an appraisal. It costs money, but shows that you are serious about helping them market their home properly. Educate your sellers about your pricing strategy, and anticipate their every question. Your answers will establish the trust and confidence needed to get through the sale as smoothly as possible.

## DISCLOSURE STATEMENTS

What if your seller lets you know that her house has what she believes to be lead paint on the interior windows? Or that there is an old underground oil tank in the backyard? *Caveat emptor* ("let the buyer beware") used to be the law for real estate transactions. Unless a buyer specifically asked the seller about potential problems with the property, the seller was under no legal obligation to disclose those problems. Now, however, every state has laws concerning seller disclosure.

In addition to state law, local custom also dictates how to deal with disclosure. This is the kind of information best sought from the more experienced agents in your office. Carol Shapiro, GRI, has been in real estate since 1997, when she earned her broker's license. She now serves as Chief Executive Officer of the Eastern Middlesex (Massachusetts) Association of REALTOR®s, and stresses, "making mistakes in this business can be very costly. Understand all of the disclosure laws, and follow them carefully."

Liz Hallford Ward, an agent in Ft. Lauderdale, Florida, explains, "my company provides disclosure forms. They are a part of our standard listing package and are given to the seller at that time. If the seller prefers, I will give them 24 hours to complete the form and I then pick it up. It is not an option. If a seller will not complete a property disclosure form, I will not list the property. I fax or give the completed seller's property disclosure to a buyer, or buyers' agent, at the point they are seriously considering making an offer. If a buyer, or buyers' agent, asks for it sooner I promptly provide it."

If your firm doesn't have its own disclosure statements, you can order them from many Internet sources, such as www.uslegalforms.com/real-estate-disclosure-forms. When you are clear about what is legally required, go over each item with your seller. You may even suggest that the seller show the form to his or her attorney for review. In most states, failure to present a disclosure statement to the buyer allows the buyer to terminate a contract. It is critical that you and your seller are educated about how best to deal with legally required disclosures.

## READYING A PROPERTY FOR SALE

If a property has obvious structural or other serious concerns, bring them up to the seller before the house is shown. Your goal is not to put down their home, but rather prepare them for the realties of showing it if it has such problems. For instance, a damp basement can either turn a buyer off completely, or give him or her reason to offer considerably less than the listing price. Dampness can be caused by leaks, which are often expensive to repair. But in many cases, cleaning gutters and redirecting downspouts can reduce dampness and doesn't cost the seller any money.

Other obvious concerns include the presence of bugs and rodents. They should be completely eliminated before the house is listed, and this often can only be accomplished by hiring a professional. Get estimates, and get the job done. There are very few buyers who will overlook this problem. A leaky roof is also a big turn-off, as it can be very expensive to repair or redo. If your seller won't remedy the situation, explain that they will have to lower their price accordingly, and be up front with buyers. Consider offering a specific dollar amount (derived from an estimate) to credit the buyer at closing.

In addition to any obvious, serious concerns, the seller should focus on more minor, but still critical, maintenance issues. To keep it simple for them, come up with a list of tips, which are part of your listing presentation materials. The list must include, but is not limited to:

1. Clean the house, including windows.

2. Sweep the front walkway and steps.

3. Control clutter (remove unneeded items, and use baskets or boxes if necessary).

4. Remove sources of unpleasant odors (also suggest simmering a cup of orange juice and drop of vanilla with spices such as cinnamon, cloves, and allspice for a few minutes each morning).

5. Maintain the lawn and gardens.

6.  Fix any peeling paint.

7.  Devise a plan to control pets during showings.

8.  Display fresh flowers or a few great houseplants.

9.  Fix the doorbell if it's not functioning.

10. Pack up small valuables.

With the homeowner addressing these issues, the property is ready to be staged. Staging involves more specific changes designed to improve the look and feel of the property. Some agents perform this service for their sellers, or create a list of suggestions for their sellers to act on. Others hire a professional to do the job, and either pass the cost of staging on to the seller, or absorb it as part of their service. Whether doing it yourself or hiring a professional, remember that there are three areas to concentrate on.

The first area is the entrance to the home. The entrance is the first impression, so it is particularly important to pay attention to detail. The doormat should be new. Add color to the entrance by adding a pot of flowers or a seasonal decoration if it's winter (plastic flowers are out, but tasteful faux greenery can work).

The second area is lighting. The home should be bright. Begin with the exterior, and have any branches removed if they block windows. On the interior, suggest removing dark, busy wallpaper and dark paint or paneling with a fresh coat of white paint. Exchange dim light bulbs for higher wattages. Clean light fixtures to allow more light to shine. Add light fixtures to dark rooms. Remove heavy drapes if they block light.

The third is spaciousness. Rearrange furniture to improve traffic flow and create the illusion of more space. But that doesn't mean pushing it all against the walls. Create conversation areas, and consider placing at least one piece of furniture at an angle. If there is too much furniture, move some pieces to other areas of the home, or put them in storage. Remove clutter, such as stacks of old magazines, excess books in bookshelves, small appliances, etc.

---

ACT NOW

During your first year in real estate, write up a listing agreement and a purchase-and-sale agreement each week whether or not you have any real business. Using fictitious information, you will gain confidence and experience dealing with the forms, and not be intimidated by them when you write them up for real.

---

## READYING THE SELLER FOR SHOWINGS

When the home is ready, get the sellers prepared for the realities of living in a home that is on the market. Many sellers wish to be present for showings. They are eager to hear feedback, and like to share knowledge of their home with the potential buyers and their agents. If that is the case with your seller, show respect for his or her opinions by eliciting their thoughts on their property's highlights. Create a flyer to leave on the hall or kitchen table for prospective buyers that draws attention to those highlights.

Gain your seller's cooperation by emphasizing that showings work better without them, because they can inhibit buyers from lingering for a better look. Any offhand remark has the potential to turn off a buyer. Tell them to play it safe and stay out longer than they think is necessary. If they must be in the home, advise them to stay in one place, rather than following the buyer and his or her agent.

Some sellers request a stipulation requiring 24-hour notice to show their property. Make them aware that last-minute and same-day requests are common, and if they don't allow them, they could keep the right buyer from ever seeing their home. It is to their advantage to make it as easy to show as possible.

If your seller asks you to be present for all showings, explain how this practice limits showings. You and the buyers' agent have busy schedules. Trying to coordinate them could put a showing off for days—days in which the buyer could find another house. In addition, buyers' agents often don't feel comfortable with the selling agent present. Again, you don't want to do anything that makes the house hard to show. When you have the cooperation of the seller, the listing not only looks better, but gets a reputation with area agents as easier to show. Properties that show well, and are priced right, are the quickest to move from listing to under contract.

## To Review

✓ First-time buyers need as much information as you can give them. Educate them about the home-buying process, and if they don't already have a pre-qualification letter, offer to help them get one.

✓ Internet-savvy buyers know the market, so you need to stress the services you provide in addition to finding them listings. Once you've helped these buyers close on a property, keep them in your database. If they forward your e-mails, they've helped you with a possible referral.

✓ Consider becoming a Certified Buyer Representative (CBR). Many buyers prefer working with these agents, and those new to real estate often work exclusively with buyers for their first months or year on the job.

✓ Before you take a buyer out to look at listings, take the time to find out what they want. Interview them, and let them do most of the talking. Ask open-ended questions that make them think and respond with more than a yes or no answer.

✓ Don't overwhelm buyers with a stack of listings. Show them a few at a time, and encourage them to take notes. Give them the listings on a clipboard with a pen, all with your name embossed on them.

✓ Some buyers are facing difficult personal crises. Be prepared to listen, but don't take on the role of psychiatrist or best friend. They need to find a new home just like other buyers. It may take a little longer, but the goal is still the same.

✓ The more prepared you are for a listing presentation, the more confident you will be. Do your homework, and package the presentation attractively.

# NAIL THE SALE

---

GETTING A PROPERTY "UNDER CONTRACT," AND THEN
MOVING THE DEAL TO THE CLOSING TABLE MEANS
WORKING YOUR WAY THROUGH A LONG TO-DO LIST.
DON'T GET OVERWHELMED EITHER BY WHAT LIES
AHEAD, OR BY THE DEMANDS OF YOUR CLIENTS. THE
MORE INFORMATION YOU HAVE, AND THE MORE YOU
CONVEY TO YOUR BUYER OR SELLER, THE EASIER IT IS TO
GET THE "TO-DO'S" MOVED TO THE "DONE" LIST. AND
ONCE THEY'RE ALL MOVED, YOUR HARD WORK IS
REWARDED WITH A COMMISSION CHECK.

---

"REALTOR®s are problem solvers," says Liz Hallford Ward. In the industry just three years, Ward is already a top-selling agent. She adds, "It is my responsibility to make my client aware of all options at every step along the way." These thoughts are echoed by other successful agents across the country. Nailing the sale is about educating your buyer or seller, guiding them through the selling process, and helping solve their problems. By keeping their interest in mind at all times, you can move them from offer to contract to closing with minimum hassles, and better commission checks.

## PREPARING SELLERS FOR AN OFFER

Sellers and their agents should have a discussion about offers before the first one comes in. When you represent the sellers, educate them about the process. Explain step-by-step how an offer is presented, the types of contingencies it might contain, how you can counter an offer, and what to do about low-ball offers. Then, get their feedback. You should be very clear about the terms under which they will accept, other than price and timeframe. How long would they be willing to wait for a buyer to be pre-approved for their loan? Would they want to take the property off the market for a buyer who isn't approved? What if the buyers must sell their home in order to buy your sellers' home? Would the sellers consider offers contingent upon the successful sale of a buyer's current home?

How do your sellers anticipate their move-out will go? If they need to take their time transferring their belongings, or are worried the closing on their new home might be delayed, you can help by countering the escrow time as "close of escrow plus [number of days]." Your seller can then rent the home from the new owners by the day until they are moved out.

If you haven't already discussed it, as suggested in Step 4, have your sellers make a list of all items not considered part of the purchase price. Any items the sellers aren't attached to, but could be taken, should be listed separately. You may need such items to bargain with during negotiations. In addition, explain to your sellers that they should expect the buyers to request certain items, such as special light fixtures, area rugs, and window treatments. Liz Hallford Ward, an agent in Ft. Lauderdale, Florida, lists portable storage sheds and hot tubs as strong bargaining chips for the seller. That doesn't mean sellers have to include them, but knowing ahead of time that they may be requested helps the seller maintain composure if negotiations become difficult.

---

### HOT TIP

Liz Hallford Ward has this advice: "on occasions when the buyer wants items that clearly are personal property, for example furniture, artwork, lawnmowers, and bicycles, I insist that buyer and seller work this out on their own. This kind of negotiating should be totally removed from the real estate transaction."

---

# HELPING BUYERS MAKE AN OFFER

As soon as buyers show signs that a particular property is "the one," or close enough to "the one," suggest writing an offer. If your market is fast-moving, let them know that if they don't act quickly, someone else could get the home. However, there is a fine line between making a suggestion and giving a hard sell. The buyer might even confuse one with the other. Too much pressure, badly timed pressure, or tactlessness can kill the sale at this point, even though the buyers have decided on a house and are on the edge of putting down a deposit.

## DISCUSS THE PROPERTY

Have a discussion with the buyers that is low-key enough not to be interpreted as a hard sell. If you are not acting as a buyers' representative, the discussion will be limited by your obligations to the seller. If you are a buyer's agent, factors that the buyer should be aware of are:

✓ **Priced too high**—When a house is overpriced, and hasn't received any offers, a low offer could get a response. There is a chance that the sellers won't budge, at which time your buyer can either overpay or look for another home.

✓ **Priced too low**—When a house is listed below market value, the sellers are trying to move the house quickly (or they have an incompetent agent). An underpriced house is likely to sell at or above the asking price.

✓ **Length of time on market**—Owners may be anxious after months without selling. They may be willing to accept an offer now that they wouldn't have considered when the house was first listed.

✓ **Reduction in price**—One drop probably means the house was initially overpriced. Several drops probably mean the homeowners are anxious to sell.

✓ **Eagerness of sellers**—If the sellers are divorcing, or have fallen into default on their mortgage, they are likely to accept a lower offer if your client is in position to close the sale quickly.

✓ **Other timing factors**—Sellers may be willing to take less money if there are expenses about to come in, such as winter heating bills or property tax payments (generally due in January and July).

✓ **The competition**—Is this house likely to receive multiple offers, or are there unlikely to be other serious buyers? Is the market for this type of property hot, or is it likely to remain unsold if these particular buyers fall through?

## FORMULATE THE OFFER

Deciding on an offering price means weighing how much the buyer can afford against the lowest price you think the sellers will accept. The outcome of the equation should be a number that is easily defendable. You don't want the buyer to get hooked on a figure that you can't explain to the sellers and their agent.

For instance, a property is listed for $200,000, has not received another offer, and needs new windows. After fielding some estimates on the windows, you determine that the replacement cost would be approximately $25,000. That means an offer of $175,000 can be explained as bearing the cost of the windows. Remind the buyer that when making a lower offer, it is best to keep the contingencies to a minimum. A number that would be accepted on its own could be rejected by insulted sellers who don't want to throw in the refrigerator and the drapes, too.

But that doesn't mean you shouldn't include contingencies. They could seal the deal later on when the seller wants to negotiate. Again, educating your client is the best way to proceed. Explain that once in the negotiation stage, the seller might think the offer is low, but be willing to take it if the buyer is flexible about the time of the closing or inclusion of the pool equipment. With an eager seller or a slow market, buyers can ask for many contingencies without seeming unreasonable. But if the market is hot or the house has multiple offers, the sellers may not want to be bothered with a lot of contingencies, and may sell the house to the bidder who presents the least complicated offer, even if it's slightly below the highest offer.

Help your buyer to understand how to weigh the condition of the house, the market, the listing price, and the sellers' frame of mind, to come up with an offer. Of course, as with setting a listing price, the buyer has the final say. It is your job to educate and be professional, but the money is theirs to spend.

# PRESENTING OFFERS

After two decades of fielding offers, Brenda Eager explains the most important step in the process. "Before you ever present an offer to your seller, you need to understand the financial qualifications of the buyer. Read pre-qualification letters carefully. Buyers can get them from the Internet, or even from a local lender, without a credit check or income verification. That makes them worthless. You must be able to interpret these letters to determine which are valid and which aren't. It's always better to go with a buyer who is pre-approved, rather than pre-qualified."

## PRESENTING TO YOUR SELLERS

Often how you present an offer is as important as the offer itself. Remember that it is your job to weed out unqualified buyers from the pack, but other than that, the seller needs to make the decision. You can help them in a number of ways. For example:

✓ **Provide context.** Explain the buyers' concerns and financial situation. Is this their first house? Are they expecting their first child? Are they "old house" people who fell in love with the charm of the sellers' antique home? Any information you can share that will encourage empathy from the seller can help in the process.

✓ **Allow them to vent their disappointment or anger at a low offer, or one with many contingencies.** But then help them deal with those feelings and move on. You might say, "I know you are angry right now. But these buyers are serious. I think we can find a solution that can work for everyone."

✓ **Don't try to convince the seller to take an offer they don't like.** First, you should never pressure them to do anything. Second, they may become suspicious of your motives. Instead, explain how a counteroffer could bring them closer to getting what they hoped for. If you've given them all the information they need to make a decision, and they still don't want to take it, move on.

✓ **Show your expertise as a strategist.** Remind the sellers that you have been through this process many, many times, and you know what works, and what doesn't. You might say, "this offer is unacceptable as written, but that doesn't mean we should walk away from it. Every offer like this should get a response. I recommend countering higher than the price you'll accept at first, to leave some room to negotiate. If the buyer counters back, you may have to come down some more."

✓ **Let them know there is a bottom line.** You won't counter and counter back endlessly. Again, stress your experience. If the buyer won't come close to a reasonable offer, tell your sellers you'll move on.

✓ **Present the offer in person.** You have much greater control over the situation if you can use not only your words, but body language and eye contact, too. In person, there is little room for misinterpretation. The telephone is your next best option, although you should be certain you have prepared the sellers properly before presenting the offer. Never present an offer via e-mail.

## DEALING WITH MULTIPLE OFFERS

Multiple offers can be great for the seller, providing the luxury of being choosy, and the chance to get what they want with very little negotiating. For the buyer, it's important to have an agent who is an aggressive negotiator. Offers need to increase or otherwise improve quickly in order to win. However, buyers who don't like competition and aggressive techniques could back away if they know other offers are on the table. Other buyers are turned off of multiple-offer situations because they assume the seller is simply trying to push up the price by claiming there are other offers when none actually exist.

Revealing the status of multiple offers is up to the seller. The fact is the buyer must wait for a response, and has no right to know if there are more offers. The National Association of REALTOR®s' Code of Ethics does however instruct its members to reveal them when asked, after seeking guidance from their clients. A Standard of Practice states that "REALTOR®s, in response to inquiries from buyers or cooperating brokers shall, with the sellers' approval, divulge the existence of offers on the property."

There are several other Standards of Practice which deal with multiple offers. First, a REALTOR®"shall submit offers and counteroffers objectively and as quickly as possible." In fact, all offers must be submitted until the seller has made a final decision. "When acting as listing brokers, REALTOR®s shall continue to submit to the seller/landlord all offers and counteroffers until closing or execution of a lease unless the seller/landlord has waived this obligation in writing. REALTOR®s shall not be obligated to continue to market the property after an offer has been accepted by the seller/landlord."

When all offers have been submitted, meet with your seller to review them. The seller can accept or begin countering more than one offer at a time, however, he or she must set an order of precedence, i.e., primary offer, first backup contract, second backup contract, etc.

Be sure to get released from an offer before finalizing the selected offer, i.e., don't sell the house twice.

## PRESENTING FOR BUYERS

If you are a buyer's representative, you will probably make the offer to the seller's agent, because most sellers' agents won't let you present it directly. As Jill Birdsall, an agent in Albany County, New York cautions, "As a seller's agent, I would never let the buyer's agent present an offer. My seller could form an emotional connection with their buyer, which could cloud the decision making process. Get any and all offers on paper. That way, they are black and white, and it's easier to see which offer is best."

But that doesn't mean you can't "sell" the offer to the seller's agent. If you simply hand over the contract, you have missed an important opportunity to present it in its best light. Explain the offer, and give the seller's agent as many tools and arguments to take back to the sellers as possible. If you convince the agent that the offer is reasonable, there's a good chance the agent can convince the sellers. (Of course, the same thing works in reverse for counteroffers, when the seller's agent needs to sell the offer to the buyer's agent.)

Always give a reason for any adjustment in price, so the other party doesn't feel that you're arbitrarily trying to pay less than what they think is fair. Instead of saying the property is overpriced, explain that, even though it's reasonable, your clients can't pay it. Some of the tools you can give to a seller's agent include explanations for:

- ✓ **Major contingencies.** For instance, an FHA (Federal Housing Administration) mortgage might require that the house have a drilled well instead of a dug well, so the seller will have to pay for a new well prior to closing. Or the buyers might ask the sellers to replace the furnace and leave the appliances in the house, because if they meet the asking price of the house they won't have enough money left over to buy new appliances.

- ✓ **Major price deductions.** If there is a serious structural or other hazardous issue that must be remedied immediately, explain that the offer had to be a little lower because the buyers need to be able to pay for the repair. The offer is lower than what might have been expected not to haggle for a lower price, but because the buyers are willing to spend some of their money on repairs that they are not asking the seller to make. Turn the focus of the discussion from the price to the money the sellers will save in potential repairs.

✓ **The positives in the offer.** The seller can lose sight of the fact that the buyer can pay cash, are pre-approved, are asking for very few contingencies, or are willing to be flexible on the closing date if they simply focus on the price. Help the seller's agent to highlight what's best about the offer that could otherwise be lost sight of if the seller simply focuses on the price.

# NEGOTIATING STRATEGIES

The path toward successful negotiations begins with your first meeting with your clients. That is when they begin to have confidence and trust in you as a professional who will look after their interests. It is very difficult to negotiate without that trust. In addition, you are also negotiating with another realtor. The more you know about his or her style, and what motivates him or her, the better you will be able to work the best deal for your client.

Negotiating begins with the offer/counteroffer stage. Buyers present an offer, and the seller can accept, reject, or counter it. This stage can last many rounds. Once the property is under contract, there are still many stages at which negotiations can be reopened. This section explains strategies that may be used for any stage, including one for closing the deal.

## Form a Relationship

Your relationships with buyers and sellers, which should be about trust and confidence, begin with honesty. Explain early in the process what should be expected. Turn your client into the most educated buyer or seller. Knowledge helps them formulate realistic expectations, and when they expect what's reasonable, they are much less likely to be disappointed.

For buyers, cover every item on the list on pages 68–69. For sellers, use your listing presentation to give them all the information they need about market conditions, necessary repairs, realities of selling for the asking price, and minimum acceptable price. Buyers and sellers should be aware before negotiations begin that the timing of offers and counteroffers can be frustrating. Buyers sometimes have to wait longer than they'd like after making an offer, and sellers should be prepared to respond quickly. The more your client knows about the process and how it works, the easier your job will be.

Many situations can cause buyers and sellers to become anxious. In some cases, their anxiety can cause deals to fall apart. But if your client trusts you, and you are appropriately reassuring, their fears can be dispelled. Counsel them about the value of being patient, and not jumping at an offer, or dismissing one quickly, either. If a client panics, they could make a decision based on fear, rather than fact. Your job is to help them slow down, calm down, and be objective before deciding anything.

Keep notes on the agents you face across the negotiating table. You might even ask other agents in your office for information. The more you know about them, the better you can anticipate their actions and reactions, and perform against them to get the best results.

---

### ACT NOW

Even if you're not a baseball fan, you've probably heard how players analyze pitchers before a game. They know which pitches are their best, and which are their worst. Past performances are examined carefully to help determine what they are likely to do in given situations. Award-winning agent Susan Sommers recommends this approach when negotiating. "Get to know how the other agent thinks. What is their negotiating style, and how do they operate? In most markets, there aren't that many realtors to learn [about] because such a small percentage of the total does most of the business."

---

## DEVELOP A PLAN

Strategize with your buyer or seller about how best to meet their objectives. The seller should know ahead of time how you will deal with low offers, not just understand that they will probably come in. How will you respond if the property gets no offers in the first few weeks it's listed? Involve the seller in the formulation of the strategy.

Buyers should be aware of current interest rates, and how they translate into monthly costs. For example, if they make an offer, and a counter offer raises the price by $5,000, the seller has added approximately $40 a month to their payment. Do they want to lose a great home over that amount? If they understand the numbers, they will be better negotiators.

## GET YOUR FACTS STRAIGHT

The more you can keep the discussion objective, that is, about the facts, the less likely your negotiations will turn emotional. Buyers' agents should be able to defend prices and contingencies with facts, such as the CMA and inspection report. Know ballpark figures for repairs that should be done. Seller's agents should also be well-versed with the CMA. If you know how and why comparable homes sold for what they did, you can defend the seller's position more strongly.

## GO FOR THE WIN-WIN

The best negotiations are the ones that end with everyone feeling like they've gotten what they wanted. It might sound contradictory, but it is in your client's best interest to keep in mind what will satisfy the other side. They will be willing to strike a deal when they feel they've gotten, or are as close as they can come to getting, their needs met.

For your client, win-win means knowing their bottom line, and never starting the negotiation process at that point (unless there is an unusual market situation in which your "best offer" is requested first). There should be room to maneuver. Use a concession to make the other side of the table feel they're really getting more than what you are offering. And always let the other side have the final word, because it makes them feel like they've won.

Win-win negotiating is also about the other agent. Chances are, you won't work for the buyer or seller again, but you will probably be on opposite sides of the table with the agent again. Let him or her know you are trustworthy, dependable, and reasonable. Don't lose your cool, or otherwise show emotion. And don't try to strong arm your way through negotiations either. The better you behave, the better chances they'll walk away with a positive impression of you, and the easier it will be to strike a deal next time.

## Keep Clients Informed

As we've said before, the more information your buyer or seller has, the less anxious they will be. Educate them about how negotiations work, and then keep them updated. Even if you have no news, call to check in with them at least once a day, especially if they have the jitters. Sellers are paying for your service, and so even though it may be difficult to say you haven't heard anything, make the call.

# GETTING TO THE CLOSING

Once the contract has been negotiated, you can begin the process of moving toward the closing table. As Susan Sommers, an agent for almost 20 years from Albany New York, notes, "Being 'under contract' is just the beginning. There are a huge number of steps you must take to get to the closing." And at many places along the way, the contract can be renegotiated. The most important thing you can do is be involved with each step, and make sure one follows the other as quickly as possible.

The negotiated contract typically goes first to the buyer's and seller's attorneys for review. If your client asks for advice, steer him or her to a lawyer well-versed in real estate law. You don't want the contract picked apart by a well-intentioned attorney who doesn't understand the process. If one or both attorneys want to amend or change the contract, the review process can be slow. It can even lead to renegotiation. Title searches are done by attorneys in most states; if yours is one of them, check to be sure it's in the works.

---

HOT TIP

If you are working for the buyer, suggest that they interview and select an inspector as soon as a contract is accepted by both parties. Most contracts specify that the inspection take place within about a week. Since good inspectors are heavily scheduled, the sooner the buyer gets to work on this detail, the better.

---

The next step is the home inspection. Whether working for the buyer or seller, it's wise to be in attendance. In fact, all of the agents we surveyed mentioned this as their number one piece of advice regarding the inspection. If there is a problem, you can immediately begin dealing with it. For example, if your sellers find out the roof needs to be replaced or repaired, you can call a few roofing companies to get estimates quickly. Since the inspection stage offers both parties the ability to back out of the contract, it's important to be there, and to show both sides that no matter the problem, it can be fixed, even if you need to renegotiate.

The next step, if you are a buyer's representative, is dealing with the mortgage contingency. In order to get from pre-approved to approved, your client must gather and submit lots of paperwork. Ask the lender for a list of all items required for closing, and ask that status reports be sent to you either via e-mail or fax. If you can't get them to provide you with updates, call the lender at least once every few days to ensure everything is progressing well. Help your buyer stay on top of the details, especially if you notice they are disorganized.

While the mortgage is being secured, the lender will schedule an appraisal. As with the inspection, it is wise to be in attendance. The appraiser examines the property to determine if it is worth the selling price. If the appraisal comes in lower than the selling price, the buyer can get out of the contract. However, if you are present when this happens, you can suggest that the seller make a concession and renegotiate. By finding solutions quickly to satisfy both sides, you can prevent a low appraisal from ruining the deal.

### DEALING WITH A LOW APPRAISAL

An appraisal that comes in thousands of dollars below the selling price doesn't have to mean the end of the deal. If you know your options, you can still move the sale forward to closing.

- **Price Reduction.** The buyer can't get a loan unless the sale price matches or is lower than the appraisal. Sometimes the seller is willing to reduce the price to that level in order to keep the deal alive.
- **Down Payment Increase.** Some buyers are willing to put more money down, effectively making a purchase with negative equity. However, there are lenders who still won't approve a loan for such a situation.
- **Combination.** The seller can reduce the price and the buyer can increase the down payment.
- **New Appraisal.** The lender may agree to hire another appraiser to examine the property.
- **Dispute the Appraisal.** Some appraisers will reexamine the property, or use different properties as comparables. If you know the comps, you can suggest that they were not adequate, and ask that they be replaced.

The last step in the closing process is the closing itself. In some states, attorneys must be present, while in others, just the agents and their clients are needed. Once it is scheduled, contact the buyer or seller to explain the closing. Tell them what to expect, how long it will take, and any other details you feel they should know. The better they understand the process ahead of time, the more relaxed they will be.

## SERVICING BUYERS

In addition to the advice above, including attending the inspection and appraisal, and staying on top of loan details, there are other ways in which you can provide excellent service to buyers.

Think ahead for them. They're probably busy concentrating on the deal, faxing or delivering documents to their lender, and arranging to move. You can help by taking care of some of the details for them.

Give the buyers a list of the utility companies, with contact information, that service the home. On the day of the closing, services should begin in their name. In addition, provide them with contact information for a number of insurance companies (if they don't already have one). They should apply for homeowner's insurance before the closing.

Counsel them to plan on moving in a few days after the closing. Sometimes the seller is slow in leaving, or repairs need to take place while the home is vacant. This time can also be used to thoroughly clean the home. If the buyer can afford it, suggest they hire a maintenance company. Provide them with a list of reliable companies that offer many services, such as rug shampooing and window washing. The more advice and information you give your buyers, the more they will appreciate your services.

## GETTING SELLERS TO THE TABLE

As the seller's agent, you will need to keep informed as to the progress being made. That means being on the phone on a regular basis with your client and with the buyer's agent. Make up a checklist of important dates, such as the appraisal and inspection cut-offs, loan contingency, etc. If any step is late, call and ask why.

If you haven't attended the inspection, find out the results immediately. If the inspection report lists many problems, and the buyers are asking for concessions, remind your sellers that the report is not a wish list. Your contract probably specifies which systems should be in good working order at closing. For instance, if the furnace is older, but still functions, it is in good working order. If it has a leak, and it is repairable, the furnace will be in good working order. Just because the buyer is demanding that the seller replace it doesn't mean they are contractually obligated to do so.

The contract may also state that the seller is not obligated to make any repairs. However, holding firm to such as position could backfire if the buyer is making a reasonable request. Rather than let the deal fall through, it may be worth spending some money on repairs. Remind your clients that they should arrange to have utilities shut off the night before or morning of the closing. If they are selling one property and moving to another, they expect the two closings to happen on the same day, or as close to the same day as possible. If you are handling both transactions, you will need to make sure the timing is right. If not, you have two different agents to communicate with.

---

### BEFORE THE CLOSING: A CHECKLIST

✓ **Double-check every detail.** Be sure that you have all required paperwork, and that it is filled out properly. Has every last-minute item, such as working out the oil adjustment if the house has oil heat, been taken care of? Is the required insurance in place?

✓ **Make sure the property is ready for the walk-through.** Check it yourself, to be certain everything the sellers promised to do is done.

✓ **Ascertain that the buyers have all the money they need to close, in an appropriate form.** Check their numbers to see if they've miscounted, or written an amount in wrong.

✓ **Check with the lender and the lawyer (if there is one) to make sure that everything is in order, and nobody has written the wrong time on their schedule.** Make sure the lender will be in his or her office during the closing in case you need to call to fix a last-minute hitch.

✓ **Make certain that the buyer and seller know where they're supposed to be, and at what time.** Give people directions if they need them. If either party has a history of lateness, you may want to arrange to pick them up and take them to the closing, or give them a starting time half an hour before the actual scheduled closing. If they question the time change, simply tell them that you need to go over documents with them.

✓ **If your clients have children or elderly parents, make sure they have arranged for care for longer than the anticipated closing time.** If there's a problem and the closing takes six hours, you want your client to be able to concentrate on getting the problem solved, not on who's watching the kids.

✓ **Reassure both buyer and seller that everything is going well, and that this is a fair deal for both sides.** Do what you can to soothe any tensions or calm any pre-closing jitters.

# THE DAY OF THE CLOSING

Before the closing, buyers and their agents conduct one last inspection, referred to as the walk through. It is intended to assure that the house is as agreed on, and all conditions have been met. If the sellers want to be present, speak with their agent and try to discourage them. Tension could be high, and you don't want any last-minute misunderstandings or sparks flying.

If you represent the buyers, arrange to meet them just before the walk through. Make sure they've had coffee or juice and are not grumpy from low blood sugar. Be upbeat but don't overdo it; this is a serious commitment for the buyers and they're likely to be in a serious mood.

If the buyers or sellers are not morning people, avoid chatter. Answer their questions, but follow their cue about how much to talk. Don't feel the need to fill pauses or silences in the conversation; many people prefer quiet first thing in the morning.

If a problem arises, concentrate on fixing it, rather than laying blame or panicking at the potential consequences. At this point, things are pretty far along. A major problem might make for a long, frustrating closing. It might mean all parties (and their agents) have to make some last-minute concessions to get things done. But it's unlikely to kill the sale at this point if you address it promptly rather than trying to lay blame.

## At the Table

You and your clients have made it to the final step. If anything goes wrong at this point, it is usually a personality issue. Help everyone to focus on getting the deal done, rather than how they feel about one another. To keep the closing running smoothly:

✓ **Make sure all the paperwork is there and no one has forgotten anything.** If possible, stop by the location of the closing a few hours early to make sure all the details are in place.

✓ **Bring extra pens and notepads for everyone;** don't assume everyone will come to closing with writing supplies. Buyers and sellers will be able to jot down any last minute details if necessary. And having a scratch pad to doodle on may help clients ease nervous tension while talking or waiting for someone else to finish rereading a document during closing.

✓ **Make sure there's coffee (or whatever each party likes to drink) and something light to nibble on.** It will ease tensions, give people something to do other than fidget, and remind them that you have their interests in mind.

✓ **Keep everything moving along.** Be friendly, but if someone gets sidetracked or starts telling unrelated stories, gently bring them back on topic. The faster the closing goes, the less chance there is that discord will surface.

✓ **If the buyer or seller has legitimate questions, make sure they're answered.** Don't try to railroad people through the sale, or make them feel stupid for not having thought of the questions earlier. A person who feels he or she is being coerced may get angry or suspicious enough to call the whole process to a halt.

✓ **If the buyer and seller have clashed earlier, make sure that you take steps to minimize the friction.** Make sure your client is not left alone; if possible you want to be with him or her to lend encouragement and to keep the focus away from his or her dislike of the other party. Buyers and sellers who don't get along should be seated at inconvenient angles to each other (such as on the same side of the table, with bankers and lawyers in between) so they can't glare at each other across the table until the tension simmers into an open fight.

## THE DOCUMENTS

For the buyer, the closing is actually two closings. They not only close on the purchase of real estate, but also on the mortgage loan they are taking to buy it. Each transaction involves a stack of paperwork. Especially for first-time or otherwise jittery buyers, it is a good idea to explain the documents ahead of time, so nerves are calmed and questions are answered ahead of time. At the table, help your clients check all figures to be sure there are no typos or other errors.

Mortgage documents include:

✓ **Truth-in-lending statement (or Regulation Z):** discloses the interest rate, annual percentage rate, amount financed, and total cost of the loan over its life.

✓ **Itemization of amount financed:** summarizes finance costs, including points.

✓ **Monthly payment letter:** breaks down the monthly payment into principal, interest, taxes, insurance, and any other monthly escrows.

✓ **Note:** acknowledges the loan, guarantees it will be paid back.

✓ **Mortgage:** puts a lien on the house as security for the loan (which means the bank can foreclose if you default on the note).

Real estate documents include:

✓ **HUD Form 1 or Disclosure/Settlement Statement:** contains the actual settlement costs and amounts.

✓ **Warranty deed:** includes the names of the buyer and the seller, and a description of the property. It may also guarantee that the seller has the right to sell the property. Upon signing by both parties, it transfers the title of property.

✓ **Proration agreements:** describe how buyer and seller are splitting the costs of the house for the month in which it is being bought. Costs may include property taxes, heating oil, and homeowners' association dues.

✓ **Tax and utility receipts:** determine who will pay for what, and when.

✓ **Acknowledgment of reports:** assures that the buyer has seen all of the reports regarding the property, including surveys and inspections.

✓ **Search or Abstract of Title:** lists all recorded documents about the property.

After the closing, it's time to get back to work. Your client should be added to your database, so you can contact him or her in the future. Begin by sending them a short note the day after the closing. Thank them for their business, and wish them happiness in their new home. Having a small flower arrangement delivered is also a good idea. Make sure your buyer or seller retains a positive impression of your services. You want them to remember you the next time they need to buy, sell, or refer a realtor!

## To Review

✓ Have a discussion with your sellers before the first offer is presented. Be certain they understand the process, and how you will represent them, and also make sure you understand them, and what they are willing to consider.

✓ As soon as buyers show serious interest in a property, suggest, without pressure, writing an offer. Make them aware of all of the information you have, and can share, such as time on the market, price (too high or too low), and eagerness of sellers. Your offer should be defendable rather than a number seemingly pulled from thin air.

Help your buyers decide on contingencies that make sense for them and won't alienate the sellers.

✓ When presenting an offer to your sellers, do it in person. Help them understand the context of the offer, including the ability of the buyers to complete the sale. Allow them to vent anger or frustration if the offer is low or complicated, but then come across as a strong negotiator who can fire back a counteroffer and make the deal work for them.

✓ If you are presenting to the sellers' agent, give him or her tools they need to sell your offer to their clients. Explain your reasoning in determining the offer, and as much background about the buyers as possible.

✓ It is important to form a positive relationship with your buyer or seller. When they like and trust you, they will have confidence in your skills as you guide them through the negotiation process. Keep them informed throughout the process.

✓ Formulate a plan with your buyers or sellers ahead of time as to how you will deal with issues such as low offers, counteroffers, and time on the market without offers.

✓ Do your homework so that you can negotiate with facts and figures.

✓ Good negotiators let the other side feel they are winning, too. Don't let the other realtor and her clients walk away feeling like they've been taken advantage of.

✓ To get to the closing table, you need to follow up on every detail. Make sure the inspection is scheduled, and attend it. Get updates on the loan status, and remind your clients of what they need to be doing next. Every few days you should be checking to see that timely progress is being made.

✓ Try to keep buyers and sellers apart on the day of the closing. Sellers don't need to be present for the walk-through, for example. Since all of the details of the sale are already worked out, the number one problem at this stage is personality issues. Distance keeps those issues from arising.

✓ After the closing, add your buyers or sellers to your database. Send a thank you note or gift, and keep in touch. Some day, they will be buyers or sellers again, and you want them to use your services again.

# POWER WORDS
# AND PHRASES

Use these words to describe houses in your listings, ads, flyers, letters, and conversations. Be specific. Find the exact word or words that convey the meaning you intend rather than using an entire sentence that simply hints at that meaning. Being precise and concise also means avoiding modifiers such as "more" and "totally," which clutter up your writing without adding substance.

## PROPERTY-SPECIFIC WORDS

| | | |
|---|---|---|
| airy | breathtaking | charming |
| amenities | bright | child-friendly |
| ample | bustling | city view |
| antique | (neighborhood) | classic |
| beachfront | captivating | clean |
| beautiful | cathedral ceilings | colonial |
| brand-new | central | comfortable |

| | | |
|---|---|---|
| community | immaculate | restored |
| conveniences | incomparable | rich |
| cozy | incredible | roomy |
| craftsmanship | lake view | rustic |
| custom | large | safe |
| delightful | lifestyle | scenic |
| desirable | lively | secluded |
| distinguished | location | security |
| dramatic | luxurious | serene |
| easy | magnificent | solid |
| easy financing | matchless | sophisticated |
| elegant | modern | southern exposure |
| excellent | new | spacious |
| exciting | open | special |
| exclusive | opportunity | spectacular |
| expansive | original | spotless |
| exquisite | outstanding | stable |
| extraordinary | panoramic view | storage |
| features | parks | strong |
| federal | peaceful | stunning |
| fine | perfect | sturdy |
| garden | preeminent | substantial |
| gem | premier | sunny |
| glamorous | prestigious | superior |
| gorgeous | pristine | terrific |
| graceful | private | ultimate |
| great location | quaint | unique |
| handsome | quality | unmatched |
| hardwood floors | quiet | unparalleled |
| haven | rare | updated/up-to-date |
| high ceilings | refuge | upscale |
| historic | remarkable | value |
| homey | remodeled | vibrant |
| ideal | renovated | victorian |

| view | waterfront | well-maintained |
| vista | well-kept | workmanship |

## General Descriptive Words

| accomplish | creative | initiate |
| accountability | customer service and | marketing |
| achieve |   satisfaction | negotiate/negotiable |
| advertising | detail-oriented | network |
| advice | develop | on-time manner |
| aggressive | driven | organized |
| analyze | dynamic | plan |
| attain | effective | prepare |
| available | efficient | proactive |
| care | effort | proven |
| careful | established | reputation |
| client's best interests | expedite | respect |
| client-focused | facilitate | responsibility |
| concern | focus | service |
| consideration | goals | track record |
| contacts | identify | value |
| coordinated | improve | x-year history |

# REAL ESTATE GLOSSARY

This glossary contains over 900 key terms that are listed in alphabetical order for easy reference.

## A

**Abstract of Title**—a certified summary of the history of a title to a particular parcel of real estate that includes the original grant and all subsequent transfers, encumbrances, and releases.

**acceleration clause**—a clause in a note, mortgage, or deed of trust that permits the lender to declare the entire amount of principal and accrued interest due and payable immediately in the event of default.

**acceptance**—the indication by a party receiving an offer that they agree to the terms of the offer. In most states the offer and acceptance must be reduced to writing when real property is involved.

**accretion**—the increase or addition of land resulting from the natural deposit of sand or soil by streams, lakes, or rivers.

**accrued depreciation**—(1) the amount of depreciation, or loss in value, that has accumulated since initial construction; (2) the difference between the current appraised value and the cost to replace the building new.

**accrued items**—a list of items of expenses that have been incurred but have not yet been paid, such as interest on a mortgage loan, that are included on a closing statement.

**acre**—a measure of land equal to 43,560 square feet or 4,840 square yards.

**actual eviction**—the result of legal action brought by a landlord against a defaulted tenant, whereby the tenant is physically removed from rented or leased property by a court order.

**actual notice**—the actual knowledge that a person has of a particular fact.

**addendum**—any provision added to a contract. Or, an addition to a contract that expands, modifies, or enhances the clarity of the agreement. To be a part of the contract and legally enforceable, an addendum must be referenced within the contract.

**adjacent**—lying near to but not necessarily in actual contact with.

**adjoining**—contiguous or attached; in actual contact with.

**Adjustable-Rate Mortgage (ARM)**—a mortgage in which the interest changes periodically, according to corresponding fluctuations in an index. All ARMs are tied to indexes. For example, a seven-year, adjustable-rate mortgage is a loan where the rate remains fixed for the first seven years, then fluctuates according to the index to which it is tied.

**adjusted basis**—the original cost of a property plus acquisition costs, plus the value of added improvements to the property minus accrued depreciation.

**adjustment date**—the date the interest rate changes on an adjustable-rate mortgage.

*ad valorem* **tax**—tax in proportion to the value of a property.

**adverse possession**—a method of acquiring title to another person's property through court action after taking actual, open, hostile, and continuous possession for a statutory period of time; may require payment of property taxes during the period of possession.

**affidavit**—a written statement made under oath and signed before a licensed public official, usually a notary public.

**agency**—the legal relationship between principal and agent that arises out of a contract wherein an agent is employed to do certain acts on behalf of the principal who has retained the agent to deal with a third party.

**agent**—one who has been granted the authority to act on behalf of another.

**alienation**—the transfer of ownership of a property to another, either voluntarily or involuntarily.

**alienation clause**—the clause in a mortgage or deed of trust that permits the lender to declare all unpaid principal and accrued interest due and payable if the borrower transfers title to the property.

**allodial system**—in the United States, a system of land ownership in which land is held free and clear of any rent or services due to the government; commonly contrasted with the Feudal system, in which ownership is held by a monarch.

**amenities**—features or benefits of a particular property that enhance the property's desirability and value, such as a scenic view or a pool.

**amortization**—the method of repaying a loan or debt by making periodic installment payments composed of both principal and interest. When all principal has been repaid, it is considered fully amortized.

**amortization schedule**—a table that shows how much of each loan payment will be applied toward principal and how much will be applied toward interest over the lifespan of the loan. It also shows the gradual decrease of the outstanding loan balance until it reaches zero.

**amortize**—to repay a loan through regular payments that are comprised of principal and interest.

**Annual Percentage Rate (APR)**—the total or effective amount of interest charged on a loan, expressed as a percentage, on a yearly basis. This value is created according to a government formula intended to reflect the true annual cost of borrowing.

**anti-deficiency law**—laws used in some states to limit the claim of a lender on default on payment of a purchase money mortgage on owner-occupied residential property to the value of the collateral.

**anti-trust laws**—laws designed to protect free enterprise and the open marketplace by prohibiting certain business practices that restrict competition. In reference to real estate, these laws would prevent such practices as price-fixing or agreements by brokers to limit their areas of trade.

**apportionments**—adjustment of income, expenses, or carrying charges related to real estate, usually computed to the date of closing so that the seller pays all expenses to date, then the buyer pays all expenses beginning on the closing date.

**appraisal**—an estimate or opinion of the value of an adequately described property, as of a specific date.

**appraised value**—an opinion of a property's fair market value, based on an appraiser's knowledge, experience, and analysis of the property based on comparable sales.

**appraiser**—an individual qualified by education, training, and experience to estimate the value of real property. Appraisers may work directly for mortgage lenders, or they may be independent contractors.

**appreciation**—an increase in the market value of a property.

**appurtenance**—something that transfers with the title to land even if it's not an actual part of the property, such as an easement.

**arbitration**—the process of settling a dispute in which the parties submit their differences to an impartial third party, on whose decision on the matter is binding.

**assessed value**—the value of a property used to calculate real estate taxes.

**assessor**—a public official who establishes the value of a property for taxation purposes.

**assessment**—the process of assigning value on property for taxation purposes.

**asset**—items of value owned by an individual. Assets that can be quickly converted into cash are considered *liquid assets*, such as bank accounts and stock portfolios. Other assets include real estate, personal property, and debts owed.

**assignment**—the transfer of rights or interest from one person to another.

**assumption of mortgage**—the act of acquiring the title to a property that has an existing mortgage and agreeing to be liable for the payment of any debt still existing on that mortgage. However, The lender must accept the transfer of liability for the original borrower to be relieved of the debt.

**attachment**—the process whereby a court takes custody of a debtor's property until the creditor's debt is satisfied.

**attest**—to bear witness by providing a signature.

**attorney-in-fact**—a person who is authorized under a power of attorney to act on behalf of another.

**avulsion**—the removal of land from one owner to another when a stream or other body of water suddenly changes its channel.

# B

**balloon mortgage**—a loan in which the periodic payments do not fully amortize the loan, so that a final payment (a balloon payment), substantially larger than the amount of the periodic payments must be made to satisfy the debt.

**balloon payment**—the final, lump-sum payment that is due at the termination of a balloon mortgage.

**bankruptcy**—an individual or individuals can restructure or relieve themselves of debts and liabilities by filing in federal bankruptcy court. There are many types of bankruptcies, and the most common for an individual is "Chapter 7, No Asset," which relieves the borrower of most types of debts.

**base line**—one of the imaginary east-west lines used as a reference point when describing property with the rectangular or government survey method of property description.

**beneficiary**—(1) one who benefits from the acts of another; (2) the lender in a deed of trust.

**bequest**—personal property given by provision of a will.

**betterment**—an improvement to property that increases its value.

**bill of sale**—a written instrument that transfers ownership of personal property. A bill of sale cannot be used to transfer ownership of real property, which is passed by deed.

**binder**—an agreement, accompanied by an earnest money deposit for the purchase of a piece of real estate, to show the purchaser's good faith intent to complete a transaction.

**biweekly mortgage**—a mortgage in which payments are made every two weeks instead of once a month. Therefore, instead of making twelve monthly payments during the year, the borrower makes the equivalent of thirteen monthly payments. The extra payment reduces the principal, thereby reducing the time it takes to pay off a thirty-year mortgage.

**blanket mortgage**—a mortgage in which more than one parcel of real estate is pledged to cover a single debt.

**bona fide**—in good faith, honest.

**bond**—evidence of personal debt secured by a mortgage or other lien on real estate.

**boot**—money or property provided to make up a difference in value or equity between two properties in an exchange.

**branch office**—a place of business secondary to a principal office. The branch office is a satellite office generally run by a licensed broker, for the benefit of the broker running the principal office, as well as the associate broker's convenience.

**breach of contract**—violation of any conditions or terms in a contract without legal excuse.

**broker**—the term *broker* can mean many things, but in terms of real estate, it is the owner-manager of a business that brings together the parties to a real estate transaction for a fee. The roles of broker and broker's associates are defined by state law. In the mortgage industry, broker usually refers to a company or individual that does not lend the money for the loans directly, but brokers loans to larger lenders or investors.

**brokerage**—the business of bringing together buyers and sellers or other participants in a real estate transaction.

**building code**—local regulations that control construction, design, and materials used in construction that are based on health and safety regulations.

**building line**—the distance from the front, rear, or sides of a building lot beyond which no structures may extend.

**buydown**—usually refers to a fixed-rate mortgage where the interest rate is bought down for a temporary period, usually one to three years. After that time and for the remainder of the term, the borrower's payment is calculated at the note rate. In order to buy down the initial rate for the temporary payment, a lump sum is paid and held in an account used to supplement the borrower's monthly payment. These funds usually come from the seller as a financial incentive to induce someone to buy their property.

**buyer's broker**—a real estate broker retained by a prospective buyer; this buyer becomes the broker's client to whom fiduciary duties are owed.

**bylaws**—rules and regulations adopted by an association, such as a condominium.

# C

**cancellation clause**—a provision in a lease that confers on one or all parties to the lease the right to terminate the parties' obligations, should the occurrence of the condition or contingency set forth in the clause happen.

**canvassing**—the practice of searching for prospective clients by making unsolicited phone calls and/or visiting homes door-to-door.

**cap**—the limit on fluctuation rates regarding adjustable rate mortgages. Limitations, or caps may apply to how much the loan may adjust over a six-month period, an annual period, and over the life of the loan. There is also a limit on how much that payment can change each year.

**capital**—money used to create income, or the net worth of a business as represented by the amount by which its assets exceed its liabilities.

**capital expenditure**—the cost of a betterment to a property.

**capital gains tax**—a tax charged on the profit gained from the sale of a capital asset.

**capitalization**—the process of estimating the present value of an income-producing piece of property by dividing anticipated future income by a capitalization rate.

**capitalization rate**—the rate of return a property will generate on an owner's investment.

**cash flow**—the net income produced by an investment property, calculated by deducting operating and fixed expenses from gross income.

*caveat emptor*—let the buyer beware [Latin].

**CC&R**—Covenants, conditions, and restrictions of a cooperative or condominium development.

**certificate of discharge**—a document used when the security instrument is a mortgage.

**certificate of eligibility**—a document issued by the Veterans Administration that certifies a veteran's eligibility for a VA loan.

**Certificate of Reasonable Value (CRV)**—once the appraisal has been performed on a property being bought with a VA loan, the Veterans Administration issues a CRV.

**certificate of sale**—the document given to a purchaser of real estate that is sold at a tax foreclosure sale.

**certificate of title**—a report stating an opinion on the status of a title, based on the examination of public records.

**chain of title**—the recorded history of conveyances and encumbrances that affect the title to a parcel of land.

city—a large municipality governed under a charter and granted by the state.

clear title—a title that is free of liens and legal questions as to ownership of a property that is a requirement for the sale of real estate; sometimes referred to as just title, good title, or free and clear.

closing—the point in a real estate transaction when the purchase price is paid to the seller and the deed to the property is transferred from the seller to the buyer.

closing costs—there are two kinds: (1) *non-recurring closing costs* and (2) *pre-paid items*. Non-recurring closing costs are any items paid once as a result of buying the property or obtaining a loan. Pre-paid items are items that recur over time, such as property taxes and homeowners insurance. A lender makes an attempt to estimate the amount of non-recurring closing costs and pre-paid items on the Good Faith Estimate, which is issued to the borrower within three days of receiving a home loan application.

closing date—the date on which the buyer takes over the property.

closing statement—a written accounting of funds received and disbursed during a real estate transaction. Buyer and seller receive separate closing statements.

cloud on the title—an outstanding claim or encumbrance that can affect or impair the owner's title.

clustering—the grouping of home sites within a subdivision on smaller lots than normal, with the remaining land slated for use as common areas.

codicil—a supplement or addition to a will that modifies the original instrument.

coinsurance clause—a clause in an insurance policy that requires the insured to pay a portion of any loss experienced.

collateral—something of value hypothecated (real property) or pledged (personal property) by a borrower as security for a debt.

collection—when a borrower falls behind, the lender contacts the borrower in an effort to bring the loan current. The loan goes to collection.

color of title—an instrument that gives evidence of title, but may not be legally adequate to actually convey title.

commission—the fee paid to a broker for services rendered in a real estate transaction.

commitment letter—a pledge in writing affirming an agreement.

common law—the body of law derived from local custom and judicial precedent.

common areas—portions of a building, land, and amenities owned (or managed) by a planned unit development or condominium project's homeowners' association or a cooperative project's cooperative corporation that are used by all of the unit owners, who share in the common expenses of their operation and maintenance. Common areas may include swimming pools, tennis courts, and other recreational facilities, as well as common corridors of buildings, parking areas, and lobbies.

community property—a system of property ownership in which each spouse has equal interest in property acquired during the marriage; recognized in nine states.

comparable sales—recent sales of similar properties in nearby areas that are used to help estimate the current market value of a property.

competent parties—people who are legally qualified to enter a contract, usually meaning that they are of legal age, of sound mind, and not under the influence of drugs or other mind-altering substances.

Competitive Market Analysis (CMA)—an analysis intended to assist a seller or buyer in determining a property's range of value.

condominium—a form of ownership in which an individual owns a specific unit in a multi-unit building and shares ownership of common areas with other unit owners.

**condominium conversion**—changing the ownership of an existing building (usually a multi-dwelling rental unit) from single ownership to condominium ownership.

**consideration**—something of value that induces parties to enter into a contract, such as money or services.

**construction mortgage**—a short-term loan used to finance the building of improvements to real estate.

**constructive eviction**—action or inaction by a landlord that renders a property uninhabitable, forcing a tenant to move out with no further liability for rent.

**constructive notice**—notice of a fact given by making the fact part of the public record. All persons are responsible for knowing the information, whether or not they have actually seen the record.

**contingency**—a condition that must be met before a contract is legally binding. A satisfactory home inspection report from a qualified home inspector is an example of a common type of contingency.

**contract**—an agreement between two or more legally competent parties to do or to refrain from doing some legal act in exchange for a consideration.

**contract for deed**—a contract for the sale of a parcel of real estate in which the buyer makes periodic payments to the seller and receives title to the property only after all, or a substantial part, of the purchase price has been paid, or regular payments have been made for one year or longer.

**conventional loan**—a loan that is neither insured nor guaranteed by an agency of government.

**conversion option**—an option in an adjustable-rate mortgage convert to to a fixed-rate mortgage

**convertible ARM**—an adjustable-rate mortgage that allows the borrower to change the ARM to a fixed-rate mortgage at a specific time.

**conveyance**—the transfer of title from the grantor to the grantee.

**cooperative**—a form of property ownership in which a corporation owns a multi-unit building and stockholders of the corporation may lease and occupy individual units of the building through a proprietary lease.

**corporation**—a legal entity with potentially perpetual existence that is created and owned by shareholders who appoint a board of directors to direct the business affairs of the corporation.

**counteroffer**—an offer submitted in response to an offer. It has the effect of rejecting the original offer.

**credit**—an agreement in which a borrower receives something of value in exchange for a promise to repay the lender.

**credit history**—a record of an individual's repayment of debt.

**cul-de-sac**—a dead-end street that widens at the end, creating a circular turnaround area.

**courtesy**—the statutory or common law right of a husband to all or part of real estate owned by his deceased wife, regardless of will provisions not recognized in community property states.

**curtilage**—area of land occupied by a building, its outbuildings, and yard, either actually enclosed or considered inclosed.

# D

**damages**—the amount of money recoverable by a person who has been injured by the actions of another.

**datum**—a specific point used in surveying.

**DBA**—the abbreviation for *doing business as.*

**debt**—an amount owed to another.

**decedent**—a person who dies.

**deed**—a written document that, when properly signed and delivered, conveys title to real property from the grantor to the grantee.

**deed-in-lieu**—a foreclosure instrument used to convey title to the lender when the borrower is in default and wants to avoid foreclosure.

**deed of trust**—a deed in which the title to property is transferred to a third party trustee to secure repayment of a loan; a three-party mortgage arrangement.

**deed restriction**—an imposed restriction for the purpose of limiting the use of land, such as the size or type of improvements to be allowed. Also called a *restrictive covenant*.

**default**—the failure to perform a contractual duty.

**defeasance clause**—a clause in a mortgage that renders it void where all obligations have been fulfilled.

**deficiency judgment**—a personal claim against a borrower when mortgaged property is foreclosed and sale of the property does not produce sufficient funds to pay off the mortgage. Deficiency judgments may be prohibited in some circumstances by anti-deficiency protection.

**delinquency**—failure to make mortgage or loan payments when payments are due.

**depreciation**—a loss in value due to physical deterioration, functional, or external obsolescence.

**descent**—the transfer of property to an owner's heirs when the owner dies intestate.

**devise**—the transfer of title to real estate by will.

**devisee**—one who receives a bequest of real estate by will.

**devisor**—one who grants real estate by will.

**discount rate**—The rate that lenders pay for mortgage funds—a higher rate is passed on to the borrower.

**directional growth**—the direction toward which certain residential sections of a city are expected to grow.

**discount point**—one percent of the loan amount charged by a lender at closing to increase a loan's effective yield and lower the fare rate to the borrower.

**dispossess**—to remove a tenant from property by legal process.

**dominant estate (tenement)**—property that includes the right to use an easement on adjoining property.

**dower**—the right of a widow in the property of her husband upon his death in non-community property states.

**down payment**—the part of the purchase price that the buyer pays in cash and is not financed with a mortgage or loan.

**dual agency**—occurs when an agent represents both parties in a transaction.

**due-on-sale clause**—a provision in a mortgage that allows the lender to demand repayment in full if the borrower sells the property that serves as security for the mortgage.

**duress**—the use of unlawful means to force a person to act or to refrain from an action against his or her will.

# E

**earnest money**—down payment made by a buyer of real estate as evidence of good faith.

**easement**—the right of one party to use the land of another for a particular purpose, such as to lay utility lines.

**easement by necessity**—an easement, granted by law and requiring court action that is deemed necessary for the full enjoyment of a parcel of land.

An example would be an easement allowing access from land-locked property to a road.

**easement by prescription**—a means of acquiring an easement by continued, open, and hostile use of someone else's property for a statuatorily defined period of time.

**easement in gross**—a personal right granted by an owner with no requirement that the easement holder own adjoining land.

**economic life**—the period of time over which an improved property will generate sufficient income to justify its continued existence.

**effective age**—an appraiser's estimate of the physical condition of a building. The actual age of a building may be different than its effective age.

**emblements**—cultivated crops; generally considered to be personal property.

**eminent domain**—the right of a government to take private property for public use upon payment of its fair market value. Eminent domain is the basis for condemnation proceedings.

**encroachment**—a trespass caused when a structure, such as a wall or fence, invades another person's land or air space.

**encumbrance**—anything that affects or limits the title to a property, such as easements, leases, mortgages, or restrictions.

**equity**—the difference between the current market value of a property and the outstanding indebtedness due on it.

**equity of redemption**—the right of a borrower to stop the foreclosure process.

**escalation clause**—a clause in a lease allowing the lessor to charge more rent based on an increase in costs; sometimes called a pass-through clause.

**escheat**—the claim to property by the state when the owner dies intestate and no heirs can be found.

**escrow**—the deposit of funds and/or documents with a disinterested third party for safekeeping until the terms of the escrow agreement have been met.

**escrow account**—a trust account established to hold escrow funds for safekeeping until disbursement.

**escrow analysis**—annual report to disclose escrow receipts, payments, and current balances.

**escrow disbursements**—money paid from an escrow account.

**estate**—an interest in real property. The sum total of all the real property and personal property owned by an individual.

**estate for years**—a lease hold estate granting possession for a definite period of time.

**estate tax**—federal tax levied on property transferred upon death.

**estoppel certificate**—a document that certifies the outstanding amount owed on a mortgage loan, as well as the rate of interest.

*et al*—abbreviation for the Latin phrase *et alius*, meaning *and another*.

*et ux*—abbreviation for Latin term *et uxor*, meaning *and wife*.

*et vir*—a Latin term meaning *and husband*.

**eviction**—the lawful expulsion of an occupant from real property.

**evidence of title**—a document that identifies ownership of property.

**examination of title**—a review of an abstract to determine current condition of title.

**exchange**—a transaction in which property is traded for another property, rather than sold for money or other consideration.

**exclusive agency listing**—a contract between a property owner and one broker that only gives the broker the right to sell the property for a fee within a specified period of time but does not obligate the owner to pay the broker a fee if the owner produces his own buyer without the broker's assistance.

**execution**—the signing of a contract.

**executor/executrix**—a person named in a will to administer an estate. The court will appoint an administrator if no executor is named. *Executrix* is the feminine form.

**executory contract**—a contract in which one or more of the obligations have yet to be performed.

**executed contract**—a contract in which all obligations have been fully performed.

**express contract**—an oral or written contract in which the terms are expressed in words.

**extention agreement**—an agreement between mortgagor and mortgagee to extend the maturity date of the mortgage after it is due.

# F

**fair market value**—the highest price that a buyer, willing but not compelled to buy, would pay, and the lowest a seller, willing but not compelled to sell, would accept.

**Fannie Mae**—a congressionally chartered, privately owned corporation that is the nation's largest supplier of funds for home mortgages.

**Federal Housing Administration (FHA)**—an agency within the U.S. Department of Housing and Urban Development (HUD) that insures mortgage loans by FHA-approved lenders to make loans available to buyers with limited cash.

**fee simple**—most complete form of ownership of real estate.

**FHA-insured loan**—a loan insured by the Federal Housing Administration.

**fiduciary relationship**—a legal relationship with an obligation of trust, as that of agent and principal.

**finder's fee**—a fee or commission paid to a mortgage broker for finding a mortgage loan for a prospective buyer.

**first mortgage**—a mortgage that has priority to be satisfied over all other mortgages.

**fixed-rate loan**—a loan with an interest rate that does not change during the entire term of the loan.

**fixture**—an article of personal property that has been permanently attached to the real estate so as to become an integral part of the real estate.

**foreclosure**—the legal process by which a borrower in default of a mortgage is deprived of interest in the mortgaged property. Usually, this involves a forced sale of the property at public auction, where the proceeds of the sale are applied to the mortgage debt.

**forfeiture**—the loss of money, property, rights, or privileges due to a breach of legal obligation.

**franchise**—in real estate, an organization that lends a standardized trade name, operating procedures, referral services, and supplies to member brokerages.

**fraud**—a deliberate misstatement of material fact or an act of omission made with deliberate intent to deceive (active fraud) or gross disregard for the truth (constructive fraud).

**front foot**—a measurement of property taken by measuring the frontage of the property along the street line.

**future interest**—ownership interest in property that cannot be enjoyed until the occurrence of some event; sometimes referred to as a household or equitable interest.

# G

**general agent**—an agent who is authorized to act for and obligate a principal in a specific range of matters, as specified by their mutual agreement.

**general lien**—a claim on all property, real and personal, owned by a debtor.

**government backed mortgage**—a mortgage that is insured by the Federal Housing Administration (FHA) or guaranteed by the Department of Veterans Affairs (VA) or the Rural Housing Service (RHS). Mortgages that are not government loans are identified as conventional loans.

**Government National Mortgage Association (Ginnie Mae)**—a government-owned corporation within the U.S. Department of Housing and Urban Development (HUD). Ginnie Mae manages and liquidates government-backed loans and assists HUD in special lending projects.

**government survey system**—a method of land description in which meridians (lines of longitude) and base lines (lines of latitude) are used to divide land into townships and sections.

**grant**—the transfer of title to real property by deed.

**grant deed**—a deed that includes three warranties: (1) that the owner has the right to convey title to the property, (2) that there are no encumbrances other than those noted specifically in the deed, and (3) that the owner will convey any future interest that he or she may acquire in the property.

**grantee**—one who receives title to real property.

**grantor**—one who conveys title to real property; the present owner.

**gross income multiplier**—A rough method of estimating the market value of an income property by multiplying its gross annual rent by a multiplier discovered by dividing the sales price of comparable properties by their annual gross rent.

**gross rent multiplier**—similar to *gross income multiplier*, except that it looks at the relationship between sales price and monthly gross rent.

**ground lease**—a lease of land only on which a tenant already owns a building or will construct improvements.

**guaranteed sale plan**—an agreement between a broker and a seller that the broker will buy the seller's property if it does not sell within a specified period of time.

# H

**hamlet**—a small village.

**heir**—one who is legally entitled to receive property when the owner dies intestate.

**highest and best use**—the legally permitted use of a parcel of land that will yield the greatest return to the owner in terms of money or amenities.

**holdover tenancy**—a tenancy where a lessee retains possession of the property after the lease has expired, and the landlord, by continuing to accept rent, agrees to the tenant's continued occupancy.

**Home Equity Conversion Mortgage (HECM)**—often called a reverse annuity mortgage; instead of making payments to a lender, the lender makes payments to you. It enables older homeowners to convert the equity they have in their homes into cash, usually in the form of monthly payments. Unlike traditional home equity loans, a borrower does not qualify on the basis of income but on the value of his or her home. In addition, the loan does not have to be repaid until the borrower no longer occupies the property.

**home equity line of credit**—a mortgage loan, that allows the borrower to obtain cash drawn against the equity of his home, up to a predetermined amount.

**home inspection**—a thorough inspection by a professional that evaluates the structural and mechanical condition of a property. A satisfactory home inspection is often included as a contingency by the purchaser.

**homestead**—the parcel of land and improvements legally qualifying as the owner's principal residence.

# I

**implied contract**—a contract where the agreement of the parties is created by their conduct.

**improvement**—a man-made addition to real estate.

**income capitalization approach**—a method of estimating the value of income-producing property by dividing its expected annual net operating income of the property by a capitalization rate.

**income property**—real estate developed or improved to produce income.

**independent contractor**—one who is retained by another to perform a certain task and is not subject to the control and direction of the hiring person with regard to the end result of the task. Individual contractors receive a fee for their services, but pay their own expenses and taxes and receive no employee benefits.

**index**—a number used to compute the interest rate for an adjustable-rate mortgage (ARM). The index is a published number or percentage, such as the average yield on Treasury bills. A margin is added to the index to determine the interest rate to be charged on the ARM. This interest rate is subject to any caps that are associated with the mortgage.

**inflation**—an increase in the amount of money or credit available in relation to the amount of goods or services available, which causes an increase in the general price level of goods and services.

**initial interest rate**—the beginning interest rate of the mortgage at the time of closing. This rate changes for an adjustable-rate mortgage (ARM).

**installment**—the regular, periodic payment that a borrower agrees to make to a lender, usually related to a loan.

**installment loan**—borrowed money that is repaid in periodic payments, known as installments.

**insurance**—a contract that provides indemnification from specific losses in exchange for a periodic payment. The individual contract is known as an insurance policy, and the periodic payment is known as an insurance premium.

**insurance binder**—a document that states that temporary insurance is in effect until a permanent insurance policy is issued.

**insured mortgage**—a mortgage that is protected by the Federal Housing Administration (FHA) or by private mortgage insurance (PMI). If the borrower defaults on the loan, the insurer must pay the lender the insured amount.

**installment contract**—see *contract for deed.*

**installment sale**—a transaction in which the sales price is paid to the seller in two or more installments over more than one calendar year.

**interest**—a fee charged by a lender for the use of the money loaned; or a share of ownership in real estate.

**interest accrual rate**—the percentage rate at which interest accrues on the mortgage.

**interest rate**—the rent or rate charged to use funds belonging to another.

**interest rate buydown plan**—an arrangement where the property seller (or any other party) deposits money to an account so that it can be released each month to reduce the mortgagor's monthly payments during the early years of a mortgage. During the specified period, the mortgagor's effective interest rate is bought down below the actual interest rate.

**interest rate ceiling**—the maximum interest rate that may be charged for an adjustable-rate mortgage (ARM), as specified in the mortgage note.

**interest rate floor**—the minimum interest rate for an adjustable-rate mortgage (ARM), as specified in the mortgage note.

**intestate**—to die without having authored a valid will.

**invalid**—not legally binding or enforceable.

**investment property**—a property not occupied by the owner.

# J

**joint venture**—an agreement between two or more parties to engage in a specific business enterprise.

**joint tenancy**—co-ownership that gives each tenant equal interest and equal rights in the property, including the right of survivorship.

**judgment**—a decision rendered by court determining the rights and obligations of parties to an action or lawsuit.

**judgment lien**—a lien on the property of a debtor resulting from a court judgment.

**judicial foreclosure**—a proceeding that is handled as a civil lawsuit and conducted through court, used in some states.

**jumbo loan**—a loan that exceeds Fannie Mae's mortgage amount limits. Also called a nonconforming loan.

**junior mortgage**—any mortgage that is inferior to a first lien and that will be satisfied only after the first mortgage; also called a secondary mortgage.

# L

**laches**—a doctrine used by a court to bar the assertion of a legal claim or right, based on the failure to assert the claim in a timely manner.

**land**—the earth from its surface to its center of the earth, and the air space above it.

**lease**—a contract between a landlord and a tenant wherein the landlord grants the tenant possession and use of the property for a specified period of time and for a consideration.

**leased fee**—the landlord's interest in a parcel of leased property.

**lease option**—a financing option that allows homebuyers to lease a home with an option to buy. Each month's rent payment may consist of rent, plus an additional amount that can be applied toward the down payment on an already specified price.

**leasehold**—a tenant's right to occupy a parcel of real estate for the term of a lease.

**lessee**—the one who receives that right to use and occupy the property during the term of the leasehold estate.

**lessor**—the owner of the property who grants the right of possession to the lessee.

**leverage**—the use of borrowed funds to purchase an asset.

**levy**—to assess or collect a tax.

**license**—(1) a revocable authorization to perform a particular act on another's property, (2) authorization granted by a state to act as a real estate broker or salesperson.

**lien**—a legal claim against a property to secure payment of a financial obligation.

**life estate**—a freehold estate in real property limited in duration to the lifetime of the holder of the life estate or another specified person.

**life tenant**—one who holds a life estate.

**listing agreement**—a contract between the owner and a licensed real estate broker where the broker is employed to sell real estate on the owner's terms within a given time, for which service the owner agrees to pay the broker an agreed-upon fee.

**listing broker**—a broker who contracts with a property owner to sell or lease the described property; the listing agreement typically may provide for the broker to make the property available through a multiple listing system.

**littoral rights**—a landowner's claim to use water in large, navigable lakes and oceans adjacent to property; ownership rights to land bordering bodies of water up to the high-water mark.

**loan**—a sum of borrowed money, or principal, that is generally repaid with interest.

**loan officer**—or lender, serves several functions and has various responsibilities, such as soliciting loans; a loan officer both represents the lending institution and represents the borrower to the lending institution.

**lock-in**—an agreement in which the lender guarantees a specified interest rate for a certain amount of time.

**lock-in period**—the time period during which the lender has guaranteed an interest rate to a borrower.

# M

**margin**—the difference between the interest rate and the index on an adjustable-rate mortgage. The margin remains stable over the life of the loan, while the index fluctuates.

**market data approach**—a method of estimating the value of a property by comparing it to similar properties recently sold and making monetary adjustments for the differences between the subject property and the comparable property.

**market value**—the amount that a seller may expect to obtain for merchandise, services, or securities in the open market.

**mechanic's lien**—a statutory lien created to secure payment for those who supply labor or materials for the construction of an improvement to land.

**metes and bounds**—a method of describing a parcel of land using direction and distance.

**mill**—one-tenth of one cent; used by some states to express or calculate property tax rates.

**modification**—the act of changing any of the terms of the mortgage.

**month-to-month tenancy**—tenancy in which the tenant rents for only one month at a time.

**mortgage**—a written instrument that pledges property to secure payment of a debt obligation as evidenced by a promissory note. When duly recorded in the public record, a mortgage creates a lien against the title to the property.

**mortgage banker**—an entity that originates, funds, and services loans to be sold into the secondary money market.

**mortgage broker**—an entity that, for a fee, brings borrowers together with lenders.

**mortgage lien**—an encumbrance created by recording a mortgage.

**mortgagee**—the lender who benefits from the mortgage.

**mortgagor**—the borrower who pledges the property as collateral.

**multidwelling units**—properties that provide separate housing units for more than one family that secure only a single mortgage. Apartment buildings are also considered multidwelling units.

**Multiple Listing Service (MLS)**—method of marketing a property listing to all participants in the MLS.

# N

**negative amortization**—occurs when an adjustable-rate mortgage is allowed to fluctuate independently of a required minimum payment. A gradual increase in mortgage debt happens when the monthly payment is not large enough to cover the entire principal and interest due. The amount of the shortfall is added to the remaining balance to create negative amortization.

**net listing**—a listing in which the broker's fee is established as anything above a specified amount to be received by the seller from the sale of the property.

**net worth**—the value of all of a person's assets.

**no cash-out refinance**—a refinance transaction in which the new mortgage amount is limited to the sum of the remaining balance of the existing first mortgage.

**non-liquid asset**—an asset that cannot easily be converted into cash.

**note**—a promise to repay an obligation; an "IOU" that defines how a loan will be repaid.

**note rate**—the interest rate on a promissory note.

**notice of default**—a formal written notice to a borrower that a default has occurred on a loan and that legal action may be taken.

**non-conforming use**—a use of land that is permitted to continue, or grandfathered, even after a zoning ordinance is passed that prohibits the use.

**notarize**—to attest or certify by a notary public.

**novation**—the substitution of a new contract for an existing one; the new contract must reference the first and indicate that the first is being replaced and no longer has any force and effect.

# O

**obligee**—a person whose favor on which an obligation is entered.

**obligor**—a person who is bound to another by an obligation.

**obsolescence**—a loss in the value of a property due to functional or external factors.

**offer**—to propose as payment; bid on property.

**offer and acceptance**—two of the necessary elements for the creation of a contract.

**open-end mortgage**—a loan containing a clause that allows the borrower to borrow additional funds from the lender, up to a specified amount, without rewriting the mortgage.

**option**—an agreement that gives a prospective buyer the right to purchase a seller's property within a specified period of time for a specified price.

**optionee**—one who receives or holds an option.

**optionor**—one who grants an option; the property owner.

**ordinance**—a municipal regulation.

**original principal balance**—the total amount of principal owed on a loan before any payments are made; the amount borrowed.

**origination fee**—the amount charged by a lender to cover the cost of assembling the loan package and originating the loan.

**owner financing**—a real estate transaction in which the property seller provides all or part of the financing.

# P

**package mortgage**—a mortgage that pledges both real and personal property as collateral to secure repayment of a loan.

**parcel**—a lot or specific portion of a large tract of real estate.

**participation mortgage**—a type of mortgage in which the lender receives a certain percentage of the income or resale proceeds from a property, as well as interest on the loan.

**partnership**—an agreement between two parties to conduct business for profit. In a partnership, property is owned by the partnership, not the individual partners, so partners cannot sell their interest in the property without the consent of the other partners.

**payee**—one who receives payment from another.

**payor**—one who makes payment to another.

**percentage lease**—a lease in which the rental rate is based on a percentage of the tenant's gross sales. This type of lease is most often used for retail space.

**periodic estate**—tenancy that automatically renews itself until either the landlord or tenant gives notice to terminate it.

**personal property (heraditaments)**—all items that are not permanently attached to real estate; also known as chattels.

**physical deterioration**—a loss in the value of a property due to impairment of its physical condition.

**PITI**—principal, interest, taxes, and insurance—components of a regular mortgage payment.

**Planned Unit Development (PUD)**—a type of zoning that provides for residential and commercial uses within a specified area.

**plat**—a map of subdivided land showing the boundaries of individual parcels or lots.

**plat number**—a number that identifies a parcel of real estate for which a plat has been recorded in the public record.

**PMI**—private mortgage insurance.

**point of beginning**—the starting point for a survey using the metes and bounds method of description.

**point**—a point is one percent of the loan.

**power of attorney**—a legal document that authorizes someone to act on another's behalf. A power of attorney can grant complete authority or can be limited to certain acts and/or certain periods of time.

**pre-approval**—condition where a borrower has completed a loan application and provided debt, income, and savings documentation that an underwriter has reviewed and approved. A pre-approval is usually done at a certain loan amount, making assumptions about what the interest rate will actually be at the time the loan is actually made, as well as estimates for the amount that will be paid for property taxes, insurance, etc.

**prepayment**—amount paid to reduce the outstanding principal balance of a loan before the due date.

**prepayment penalty**—a fee charged to a borrower by a lender for paying off a debt before the term of the loan expires.

**pre-qualification**—a lender's opinion on the ability of a borrower to qualify for a loan, based on furnished information regarding debt, income, and available capital for down payment, closing costs, and pre-paids. Pre-qualification is less formal than pre-approval.

**prescription**—a method of acquiring an easement to property by prolonged, unauthorized use.

**primary mortgage market**—the financial market in which loans are originated, funded, and serviced.

**prime rate**—the short-term interest rate that banks charge to their preferred customers. Changes in prime rate are used as the indexes in some adjustable-rate mortgages, such as home equity lines of credit.

**principal**—(1) one who authorizes another to act on his or her behalf, (2) one of the contracting parties to a transaction, (3) the amount of money borrowed in a loan, separate from the interest charged on it.

**principal meridian**—one of the 36 longitudinal lines used in the rectangular survey system method of land description.

**probate**—the judicial procedure of proving the validity of a will.

**promissory note**—details the terms of the loan and is the debt instrument.

**property management**—the operating of an income property for another.

**property tax**—a tax levied by the government on property, real or personal.

**prorate**—to divide ongoing property costs such as taxes or maintenance fees proportionately between the buyer and seller at closing.

**pur autre vie**—a phrase meaning *for the life of another*. In a life estate *pur autre vie*, the term of the estate is measured by the life of a person other than the person who holds the life estate.

**purchase agreement**—A written contract signed by the buyer and seller stating the terms and conditions under which a property will be sold.

**purchase money mortgage**—A mortgage given by a buyer to a seller to secure repayment of any loan used to pay part or all of the purchase price.

# Q

**qualifying ratios**—calculations to determine whether a borrower can qualify for a mortgage. There are two ratios. The "top" ratio is a calculation of the borrower's monthly housing costs (principle, taxes, insurance, mortgage insurance, homeowner's association fees) as a percentage of monthly income. The "bottom" ratio includes housing costs as well as all other monthly debt.

**quitclaim deed**—conveyance where the grantor transfers without warranty or obligations whatever interest or title he/she may have.

# R

**real estate**—land, the earth below it, the air above it, and anything permanently attached to it.

**real estate agent**—a real estate broker who has been appointed to market a property for and represent the property owner (listing agent), or a broker who has been appointed to represent the interest of the buyer (buyer's agent).

**real estate board**—organization whose members are primarily comprised of real estate sales agents, brokers, and administrators.

**real estate broker**—a licensed person, association, partnership, or corporation who negotiates real estate transactions for others for a fee.

**Real Estate Settlement Procedures Act (RESPA)**—a consumer protection law that requires lenders to give borrowers advance notice of closing costs and prohibits certain abusive practices against buyers using federally related loans to purchase their homes.

**real property**—the rights of ownership to land and its improvements.

REALTOR®—a registered trademark for use by members of the National Association of REALTOR®s and affiliated state and local associations.

recording—entering documents, such as deeds and mortgages, into the public record to give constructive notice.

rectangular survey system—a method of land description based on principal meridians (lines of longitude) and base lines (lines of latitude). Also called the government survey system.

redemption period—the statutory period of time during which an owner can reclaim foreclosed property by paying the debt owed plus court costs and other charges established by statute.

refinance transaction—the process of paying off one loan with the proceeds from a new loan using the same property as security or collateral.

release clause—a clause in a mortgage that releases a portion of the property upon payment of a portion of the loan.

remainder estate—a future interest in an estate that takes effect upon the termination of a life estate.

remaining balance—in a mortgage, the amount of principal that has not yet been repaid.

remaining term—the original amortization term minus the number of payments that have been applied to it.

rent—a periodic payment paid by a lessee to a landlord for the use and possession of leased property.

replacement cost—the current cost of replacing a building.

reproduction cost—the cost of building an exact duplicate of a building at current prices.

restriction or restrictive covenant—provisions that place limitations on the way a property can be used.

**reversion**—the return of interest or title to grantor of a life estate.

**reverse annuity mortgage**—a type of mortgage where a homeowner receives monthly checks or lump sum with no repayment until the property is sold; usually an agreement between mortgagor and elderly homeowners.

**revision**—a revised or new version, as in a contract.

**right of egress** or **ingress**—the right to enter or leave designated premises.

**right of first refusal**—the right of a person to have the first opportunity to purchase property before it is offered to anyone else.

**right of redemption**—the statutory right to reclaim ownership of property after a foreclosure sale.

**right of survivorship**—in joint tenancy, the right of survivors to acquire the interest of a deceased joint tenant.

# S

**safety clause**—a contract provision that provides a time period following expiration of a listing agreement during which the agent will be compensated if there is a transaction with a buyer who was initially introduced to the property by the agent.

**sale-leaseback**—a transaction where the owner sells improved property, and, as part of the same transaction, signs a long-term lease to remain in possession of its premises, thus becoming the tenant of the new owner.

**sales contract**—a contract between a buyer and a seller outlining the terms of the sale.

**salesperson**—one who is licensed to sell real estate in a given territory,

**salvage value**—the value of a property at the end of its economic life.

**satisfaction**—an instrument acknowledging that a debt has been paid in full.

**second mortgage**—a mortgage that is in less than the first lien position; see *junior mortgage*.

**section**—as used in the rectangular survey system, an area of land measuring one square mile, or 640 acres.

**secured loan**—a loan that is backed by property or collateral.

**security**—Property that is offered as collateral for a loan.

**selling broker**—the broker who secures a buyer for a listed property; the selling broker may be the listing agent, a subagent, or a buyer's agent.

**servient tenement**—a property on which an easement or right-of-way for an adjacent (dominant) property passes.

**setback**—the amount of space between the lot line and the building line, usually established by a local zoning ordinance or restrictive covenants (deed restrictions).

**settlement statement (HUD-1)**—the form used to itemize all costs related to the closing of a residential transaction covered by RESPA regulations.

**severalty**—the ownership of a property by only one legal entity.

**special assessment**—a tax levied against only the specific properties that will benefit from a public improvement, such as a street or sewer; an assessment by a homeowners' association for a capital improvement to the common areas for which no budgeted funds are available.

**special warranty deed**—a deed in which the grantor guarantees the title only against the defects that may have occurred during the grantor's ownership, and not against any defects that occurred prior to that time.

**specific lien**—a lien, such as a mortgage, that attaches to one defined parcel of real estate.

**standard payment calculation**—a method used to calculate the monthly payment required to repay the remaining balance of a mortgage in equal installments over the remaining term of the mortgage at the current interest rate.

**straight-line depreciation**—a method of computing depreciation by decreasing value by an equal amount each year during the useful life of the property.

**statutory lien**—a lien imposed on property by statute, such as a tax lien.

**subdivision**—a tract of land divided into lots as defined in a publicly recorded plat that complies with state and local regulations.

**sublet**—the act of a lessee transferring part or all of his or her lease to a third party while maintaining responsibility for all duties and obligations of the lease contract.

**subordinate**—by contract, to voluntarily accept a lower priority lien position than that to which one would normally be entitled.

**substitution**—the principle in appraising that a buyer will be willing to pay no more for the property being appraised than the cost of purchasing an equally desirable property.

**subrogation**—the substitution of one party into another's legal role as the creditor for a particular debt.

**suit for possession**—a lawsuit filed by a landlord to evict a tenant who has violated the terms of the lease or retained possession of the property after the lease expired.

**survey**—a map that shows the exact legal boundaries of a property, the location of easements, encroachments, improvements, rights of way, and other physical features.

# T

**tax deed**—an instrument given to the purchaser at the time of sale in some states.

**tax lien**—a charge against a property created by law or statue; tax liens take priority over all other types of liens.

**tax rate**—the rate applied to the assessed value of a property to determine the property taxes.

**tax sale**—the court-ordered sale of a property after the owner fails to pay *ad valorem* taxes owed on the property.

**tenancy at sufferance**—the tenancy of a party who unlawfully retains possession of a landlord's property after the term of the lease has expired.

**tenancy at will**—an indefinite tenancy that can be terminated by either the landlord or the tenant at any time by giving notice to the other party one rental period in advance of the desired termination date.

**tenancy by the entirety**—ownership by a married couple of property acquired during the marriage with right of survivorship; not recognized by community property states.

**tenancy in common**—a form of co-ownership in which two or more persons hold an undivided interest in property without the right of survivorship.

**tenant**—one who holds or possesses the right of occupancy title.

**tenement**—space that may be occupied by a tenant under the terms of a lease.

**testate**—to die having created a valid will directing the testator's desires with regard to the disposition of the estate.

**timesharing**—undivided ownership of real estate for only an allotted portion of a year.

**title**—a legal document that demonstrates a person's right to or ownership of a property. Note:

title is *not* an instrument. The instrument, such as a deed, gives evidence of title or ownership.

**title insurance**—an insurance policy that protects the holder from defects in a title, subject to the exceptions noted in the policy.

**title search**—a check of public records to ensure that the seller is the legal owner of the property and that there are no liens or other outstanding claims.

**Torrens system**—a system of establishing clear title and issuing title certificates to land through a governmental authority.

**township**—a division of land, measuring six miles square (36 square miles), in the government survey system.

**transfer tax**—state or municipal tax payable when the conveyancing instrument is recorded.

**trust**—an arrangement in which title to property is transferred from a grantor to a trustee, who holds title but not the right of possession for a third party, the beneficiary.

**trustee**—a person who holds title to property for another person designated as the beneficiary.

**Truth-in-Lending Law**—also known as Regulation Z; requires lenders to make full disclosure regarding the terms of a loan.

# U

**underwriting**—the process of evaluating a loan application to determine the risk involved for the lender.

**undivided interest**—the interest of co-owners to use of an entire property despite the fractional interest owned.

**unilateral contract**—a one-sided contract in which one party is obligated to perform a particular act completely, before the other party has any obligation to perform.

**unsecured loan**—a loan that is not backed by collateral or security.

**useful life**—the period of time a property is expected to have economic utility.

**usury**—the practice of charging interest at a rate higher than that allowed by law.

# V

**VA-guaranteed loan**—a mortgage loan made to a qualified veteran that is guaranteed by the Department of Veterans Affairs.

**valid contract**—an agreement that is legally enforceable and binding on all parties.

**valuation**—estimated worth.

**variable rate**—an interest rate that increases or decreases periodically in relation to an index.

**variance**—permission obtained from zoning authorities to build a structure that is not in complete compliance with current zoning laws. A variance does not permit a non-conforming use of a property.

**vendee**—a buyer.

**vendor**—a seller; the property owner.

**village**—an incorporated minor municipality usually larger than a hamlet and smaller than a town.

**void contract**—a contract that is not legally enforceable; the absence of a valid contract.

**voidable contract**—contract that appears to be valid but is subject to cancellation by one or both of the parties.

# W

**waiver**—the surrender of a known right or claim.

**walk-through inspection**—a physical examination of the property which usually takes place just before the closing to ensure that no changes have taken place, no fixtures included in the sale have been removed, and no new damage has been done to the property.

**warranty deed**—a deed in which the grantor fully warrants a good clear title to the property.

**water rights**—the legal right to use water from a water course or body of water on a property.

**will**—a written document that directs the distribution of a deceased person's property, real and personal.

**wetlands**—lands restricted for development as a result of their proximity to bodies of water and the fact that they are occasionally or often flooded; may also be environmentally sensitive.

**wraparound mortgage**—a mortgage that includes the remaining balance on an existing first mortgage plus an additional amount. Full payments on both mortgages are made to the wraparound mortgagee who then forwards the payments on the first mortgage to the first mortgagee.

# X-Y-Z

**yield**—the interest earned by an investor on his investment (also known as the *return*).

**zero lot line**—a zoning regulation that allows the positioning of a structure on a lot so that one side rests directly on the lot's boundary line (no set back).

**zone**—an area reserved by authorities for specific use that is subject to certain restrictions.

**zoning ordinance**—the exercise of regulating and controlling the use of a property in a municipality.

# RESOURCES

This listing of books, periodicals, and industry associations was complied using suggestions from the realtors interviewed for this book. It is not meant to be exhaustive, but rather is a selection of favorites used by top-selling agents around the country.

## BOOKS

### GENERAL

*Dictionary of Real Estate Terms*, Jack P. Friedman, et al. (Barron's Educational Series; 6th ed., 2004).

*The Millionaire Real Estate Agent*, Gary Keller, et al. (McGraw-Hill, 2004).

*The 90 Second Lawyer Guide to Buying Real Estate*, Robert Irwin (Wiley, 1997).

*Real Estate Agent's Business Planning Guide*, Carla Cross (Real Estate Educators Assn. 1994).

*Real Estate Essentials: A Glossary and Study Guide*, Ralph Tamper, et al. (LearningExpress, 2002).

*Real Estate Market Analysis: A Case Study Approach*, Adrienne Schmitz (Urban Land Institute, 2001).

*Real Estate Handbook*, Jack C. Harris (Barron's Educational Series; 5th ed., 2001).


## INTERNET

*One Day Course: Real Estate Internet Skills*, Curt Robbins (DDC Publishing, Inc., 1999).

*Virtual Reality: A Guide to the Internet for Real Estate and Ancillary Professionals*, Lori Robertson, Brian C. Wadell (Hollis Publishing Co., 1996).

*The Essential Internet Guide for the Real Estate Professional*, Neal Otto ( Jump-Start Computer Services, 1996).


## NEGOTIATING

*Closing the Deal*, Edward Farthing, Leigh Ronald Grossman (Learning Express, 2001).

*Negotiating & Drafting Real Estate Documents: Converting the Deal Into a Contract*, Suzanne L. King (Massachusetts Continuing Legal Education, Inc., 1999).

*Tips and Traps When Negotiating Real Estate*, Robert Irwin (McGraw-Hill, 1995).


## MARKETING

*The Manager's Guide to Real Estate Marketing*, Hal Kahn (Real Estate Brokerage, 1989).

*Real Estate Rainmaker® : Successful Strategies for Real Estate Marketing,* Dan
Gooder Richard (Wiley, 1999).
*Web Marketing for the Real Estate Professional,* Bill Koelzer, et al. (Prentice
Hall, 2001).

# PERIODICALS, PRINT AND ONLINE

Broker Agent Magazine: www.gotobam.com
Journal of Real Estate Practice and Education: www.aresnet.org/
ARES/pubs/jrepe/JREPE.html
Journal of Real Estate Research: http://137.151.62.168/finance/
journal/
National Mortgage News: www.nationalmortgagenews.com/
Real Estate Professional: www.therealestatepro.com
Realtor Magazine: www.realtor.org/RealtorMag/

# ASSOCIATIONS

ACCOLADE NETWORK, INC. (REAL ESTATE APPRAISER NETWORK)
National Assignment Center
415 G Street
Modesto, CA 95351
Phone: 209-522-9981
www.appraise.com

AMERICAN INDUSTRIAL REAL ESTATE ASSOCIATION
700 S. Flower, Suite 600
Los Angeles, CA 90017
Phone: 213-687-8777
www.airea.com

AMERICAN LAND TITLE ASSOCIATION
1828 L Street N.W., Suite 705
Washington, DC 20036
Phone: 202-296-3671
www.alta.org

AMERICAN PLANNING ASSOCIATION
122 S. Michigan Avenue Suite 1600
Chicago, IL 60603-6107
Phone: 312-431-9100
www.planning.org

THE AMERICAN REAL ESTATE SOCIETY (ARES)
College of Business and Public Administration
Gamble Hall, Room 160A
University of North Dakota
P.O. Box 7120
Grand Forks, ND 58202-7120
Phone: 701-777-3670
www.aresnet.org

AMERICAN SOCIETY OF APPRAISERS
555 Herndon Parkway Suite 125
Herndon, VA 20170
Phone: 703-478-2228
www.appraisers.org

AMERICAN SOCIETY OF FARM MANAGERS AND RURAL APPRAISERS
950 S. Cherry Street, Suite 508
Denver, CO 80246
Phone: 303-758-3513
www.agri-associations.org/asfmra

AMERICAN SOCIETY OF HOME INSPECTORS
932 Lee Street, Suite 101
Des Plaines, IL 60016-6546
Phone: 800-743-ASHI
www.ashi.com

THE APPRAISAL FOUNDATION
1029 Vermont Avenue, N.W. Suite 900
Washington, DC 20005-3517
Phone: 202-347-7722
www.appraisalfoundation.org

APPRAISAL INSTITUTE
875 N. Michigan Avenue, Suite 2400
Chicago, IL 60611-1980
Phone: 312-335-4100
www.appraisalinstitute.org
E-mail: info@appraisalinstitute.org

BUILDING OWNERS AND MANAGERS ASSOCIATION INTERNATIONAL
1201 New York Avenue N.W., Suite 300
Washington, DC 20005
Phone: 202-408-2662
www.boma.org

COMMERCIAL INVESTMENT REAL ESTATE INSTITUTE
430 N. Michigan Avenue
Chicago, IL 60611
Phone: 800-621-7027
www.ccim.com

COUNCIL OF REAL ESTATE BROKERAGE MANAGERS COUNCIL
430 N. Michigan Avenue
Chicago, IL 60611-4092
Phone: 800-621-8738
www.crb.com

EMPLOYEE RELOCATION COUNCIL
1720 N Street N.W.
Washington, DC 20036
Phone: 202-857-0857
www.erc.org

ENVIRONMENTAL SYSTEMS RESEARCH INSTITUTE, INC. (GIS AND
    MAPPING SERVICES)
380 New York Street
Redlands, CA 92373-8100
Phone: 800-447-9778
www.esri.com/company/contactusa.html

HOME INSPECTIONS—USA
Home Inspection Directory Corp.
P.O. Box 1465
North Hampton, NH 03862
Phone: 877-491-2171
www.homeinspections-usa.com/contact.html

INMAN REAL ESTATE NEWS
1250 45th Street, Suite 360
Emeryville, CA 94608
Phone: 800-775-4662
www.inman.com

INSTITUTE OF REAL ESTATE MANAGEMENT
430 N. Michigan Avenue
Chicago, IL 60611-4090
Phone: 800-837-0706
www.irem.org

MORTGAGE BANKERS ASSOCIATION OF AMERICA
1125 15th Street N.W.
Washington, DC 20005
Phone: 202-861-6500
www.mbaa.org

NATIONAL ASSOCIATION OF HOME BUILDERS
1201 15th Street N.W.
Washington, DC 20005
Phone: 202-822-0200
www.nahb.com

NATIONAL ASSOCIATION OF HOME INSPECTORS
4248 Park Glen Road
Minneapolis, MN 55416
Phone: 800-448-3942
www.nahi.org

NATIONAL ASSOCIATION OF INDEPENDENT FEE APPRAISERS
7501 Murdoch Avenue
St. Louis, MO 63119
Phone: 314-781-6688
www.naifa.com

NATIONAL ASSOCIATION OF MASTER APPRAISERS
303 W. Cypress Street
San Antonio, TX 78212-0617
Phone: 800-229-6262
www.masterappraisers.com

NATIONAL ASSOCIATION OF MORTGAGE BROKERS
8201 Greensboro Drive, Suite 300
McLean, VA 22102
Phone: 703-610-9009
www.namb.org

NATIONAL ASSOCIATION OF REAL ESTATE EDITORS (NAREE)
1003 N.W. 6th Terrace
Boca Raton, FL 33486
www.naree.org

NATIONAL ASSOCIATION OF REAL ESTATE APPRAISERS
1224 North Nokomis N.E.
Alexandria, MN 56308
Phone: 320-763-7626
www.iami.org/narea.html

NATIONAL ASSOCIATION OF REAL ESTATE BROKERS
1629 K Street, N.W., Suite 602
Washington, DC 20006
Phone: 202-785-4477
www.nareb.com

NATIONAL ASSOCIATION OF REALTORS®
430 N. Michigan Avenue
Chicago, IL 60611
Phone: 312-329-8200
www.realtor.com

NATIONAL ASSOCIATION OF RESIDENTIAL PROPERTY MANAGERS
6300 Dutchman's Parkway
Louisville, KY 40205
Phone: 800-782-3452
www.narpm.org

NATIONAL PROPERTY MANAGEMENT ASSOCIATION
1108 Pinehurst Road, The Oaktree Center
Dunedin, FL 34698
Phone: 727-736-3788
www.npma.org

REAL ESTATE EDUCATORS ASSOCIATION
320 West Sabal Palm Place, Suite 150
Longwood, FL 32779
Phone: 407-831-6688
www.reea.org

REALTY TIMES
5600 W. Lovers Lane, Suite 315
Dallas, TX 75209
Phone: 214-353-6980
www.realtimes.com

WOMEN'S COUNCIL OF REALTORS®
430 N. Michigan Avenue
Chicago, IL 60611
Phone: 312-329-8483
www.wcr.org